Looming Transitions
STARTING AND FINISHING WELL IN CROSS-CULTURAL SERVICE

Amy Young

Print Edition, January 2016
Copyright © 2016 by Amy Young

All rights reserved. This book or any portion thereof may not be reproduced or used in any manner whatsoever without the express written permission of the publisher except for the use of brief quotations in a book review.

Contents

A Shuttle, A List, and A Book 1
A Bowl of Coins 5
The Stress of Endings 19
Stay Grounded in Christ 35
Laughter Revives the Soul 48
Accept That It's Going to Be Messy 59
Know Yourself 72
Start Early 87
It's Not Just About You 102
Work Out Your Grief 118
Your Unique Path 132
Acknowledgements 149
About the Author 154
Endnotes 155

Introduction

A Shuttle, A List, and A Book

To the person who does not know where he wants to go, there is no favorable wind.
– Seneca

Tears started down my cheeks. Not wanting to draw attention to them, I inched my hand from my lap up to my eyes. *Up and down. Move slowly. Don't draw attention,* I told myself. *Do not wipe from the outside of the eye, a clear giveaway you're crying. Oh, please stop running down; you're almost flowing.* It was mid-morning, so only four of us were on the shuttle bus bound for the Denver airport. I kept my eyes straight ahead, hoping my fellow travelers might think I had something in my eyes instead of guessing I was wiping tears.

The only other woman on the shuttle stood up, came over to me, sat down, and said, "You look distraught."

You look distraught. My plan had fooled only myself. I glanced at the two businessmen who seemed uncomfortable with a stranger crying in public. But not just in public, in a small and clearly defined space that we had to share until the shuttle arrived at the airport. And now the other woman had named out loud, for all to hear, what was going on with me. With almost palpable relief that they didn't have to get involved, one of the men looked away and the other studied his newspaper all the more intently. *You look distraught.* And just like that my cover

1

was blown.

I *was* distraught. In the short time left before we arrived at the terminal and were mercifully let off of the shuttle bus, I started rambling to the woman about being in transition. That I had been in the U.S. for three years after living in China for nine; that I had earned an M.A. during the three years and was now preparing to return to China; and had I mentioned, I babbled on, that before moving to China I had lived in Kansas and on this trip I was returning for yet another hello/goodbye? And while I was anticipating a time in Kansas (it was, after all, where I wanted to live if I could pick any place), I dreaded yet another goodbye. Kansas to me is the most wonderful place on earth and I'm fine, I told the woman, I'm just in the midst of transition. The words flowed out. I added, "Emotions can be so messy in transition. Thank you for your kindness. I am distressed. But I am also okay."

We got off the shuttle bus and went our separate ways. I often wonder if that event would have been seared into my memory if that woman, like the other shuttle passengers, had pretended that nothing was happening. Probably not. Her words became a stone of remembrance for me.

They created space in my soul and marked and named what was happening.

Fast forward about eight months to my transition being (mostly) over and life up and running in China. With no tears and books unpacked, I was feeling (mostly) settled. I was asked to lead a workshop on how to finish well, geared toward people who would be returning to the U.S. after having lived and taught in Asia. I jumped at the chance; fresh off my own Band-Aid-ripping-off experience, I figured I had help to share.

All I needed to do was conduct a little bit of internet research, read some articles, throw in a few personal stories, and voilà—one basically ready-made presentation. My plan went off without a hitch until I did my first internet search. Almost everything about "ending chapters" in life was related to retiring. And yes, retiring is certainly a major area for finishing well. But what

A Shuttle, A List, and A Book

about all of the transitions that we go through when an end is coming, yet life will still go on after the transition? While there might be elements of leaving a legacy—a major theme in the retirement literature—that certainly isn't a given, or even a focus, in all transitions.

The first year I presented the workshop, I pulled together a few thoughts and told myself that the problem was my late start in the search. Information was out there and I would find it. During the next year, I found a book called *Finishing Well* by Bob Buford. According to the cover, it was "based on inspiring interviews with 60 remarkable people."[1] Looking back, I can't remember how I got the impression that this was the resource I was looking for, but it also focused on retiring. Still no help for the workshop. I went back to the list of ideas I had created the first year, added more meat to them and the idea of a book began to grow. What you hold in your hands is based on the original points:

- Stay Grounded in Christ
- Laughter Revives the Soul
- Accept That It's Going to Be Messy
- Know Yourself
- Start Early
- It's Not Just About You
- Work Out Your Grief

This book is for those who will be going through a major life transition, either moving to the field or preparing to return to your "home" country. I would enjoy sitting across from you and talking about each point in person. But that conversation might be like drinking from a fire hose, and you'd leave with information and emotion overload. Instead, I recommend starting to read this book four to six months before you'll move. My goal is for you to have these ideas, mild warnings, and strategies to journey with you during this season. Even though it may be messy, choices you make *now* will make *then* a bit easier. And if

Looming Transitions

you need to get some tissues, I'm right there on the shuttle bus of life with you.

Chapter One

A Bowl of Coins

It will be like a man going on a journey, who called his servants and entrusted his wealth to them.
—*Matthew 23:14*

Before the reward there must be labor. You plant before you harvest. You sow in tears before you reap joy.
—*Ralph Ransom*

    I lived in Chengdu, Sichuan for five years before relocating to Beijing and moving into a friend's apartment. She was relocating to the U.S. after having lived and worked in China for many years. Because I was moving into what had been her apartment, we agreed I'd buy many of the basics so she wouldn't have to deal with getting rid of them and I wouldn't have to deal with tracking down new items. The August night I arrived was hot and sticky, and the sweat dripped after I lugged my heavy bags up to my third-floor apartment.
    I opened the door with excitement because the apartment was so much nicer than where I had been living. For five years I hadn't had comfortable furniture or hot running water in the kitchen. And now to be greeted by a beautiful green-striped sofa with stylish wooden legs, it was almost too much. Like entering the promised land flowing with milk, honey, and hot water. In my jet lag delirium I randomly opened closets and drawers.
    The crash you hear are my expectations colliding with reality. I found used makeup in the bathroom drawers, in addition to

Looming Transitions

Q-tips and cotton balls. Dirty throw rugs on the floors. Clothes hanging in the closets. Drawers filled with dried-up markers, dead batteries, and keys to missing locks. The refrigerator had half-empty bottles of food. The spare bedroom was so full of things I didn't know where to start. Had someone moved out or died? Shouldn't there be a difference?

I crawled into bed, but about twenty minutes later I *had* to get up to do something about the cluttered spare bedroom which was to be my office. Where would I work? How could Sally[2], a good friend, walk out and leave me with all of this crap? After working for a bit I was able to drift off to sleep. For a long time it didn't look like my home; instead it looked like I was couch surfing in someone else's home. In the upcoming weeks and months, when people asked me where I got such and such, my frequent answer was "my raptured apartment." I was living in a space that had been someone's and then it wasn't, and apparently she only had enough time to pack her bags and get out of town.

My friend Lisa once wisely said that relationships are like balloons: their shapes are influenced by inside and outside factors. The inside factors are more under your control than the outside ones, but both come together to create the shape of the balloon. Likewise, the ability to finish well before your looming transition is going to be influenced by inside and outside factors. For example, is this transition initiated by you or by others? Does it feel like the start of a dream or the end of one? Carlos Castraneda said, "We either make ourselves miserable, or we make ourselves happy. The amount of work is the same."[3] While I don't know about the amount of work being the same in misery versus happiness, I agree work is going to be involved. This book will help you with both the inside and outside influences on your balloon so that when it is time for the transition, your balloon will be able to take off without others wondering if you've been raptured.

Hearing "Well Done"

During the workshop I lead, four small bowls filled with coins

A Bowl of Coins

are passed around with instructions to "take a few." Quizzical looks and questions of *"how many is a few?"* and *"what's the catch?"* fill the room. Smiling, I repeat the instruction, struck afresh by the almost immediate wariness we feel when we face the unknown. Since many of the workshop participants know me, they feel comfortable guessing out loud that they will need to share an example for each coin they take, but examples of what? I assure them, "You won't have to use the coins to give any examples."

I invite you to pause as well, and as the bowl of coins passes by, dip your hand into the bowl and take a few. How many did you choose?

Hold the coins in the palm of your hand. Feel the weight of each coin and of all the coins as a whole. Look at the coins ... really see them. These coins represent the future, and the reality that you will not always be in transition. Hold them as I tell a familiar story.

It will be like a man going on a journey, who called his servants and entrusted his wealth to them. To one he gave five bags of gold, to another two bags, and to another one bag, each according to his ability.[4]

You are that servant. You have been entrusted with coins. You might hold two and another might hold five. But you have coins. Your future holds a change that will come to pass in the not-so-distant future, and you have been entrusted with navigating it.

Then he went on his journey. The man who had received five bags of gold went at once and put his money to work and gained five bags more. So also, the one with two bags of gold gained two more. But the man who had received one bag went off, dug a hole in the ground and hid his master's money.

You can invest your coins, or you can dig a hole in the ground; either way, your master will return.

After a long time the master of those servants returned and set-

tled accounts with them. The man who had received five bags of gold brought the other five. "Master," he said, "you entrusted me with five bags of gold. See, I have gained five more."

His master replied, "Well done, good and faithful servant! You have been faithful with a few things; I will put you in charge of many things. Come and share your master's happiness!"

The man with two bags of gold also came. "Master," he said, "you entrusted me with two bags of gold; see, I have gained two more."

His master replied, "Well done, good and faithful servant! You have been faithful with a few things; I will put you in charge of many things. Come and share your master's happiness!"

Then the man who had received one bag of gold came. "Master," he said, "I knew that you are a hard man, harvesting where you have not sown and gathering where you have not scattered seed. So I was afraid and went out and hid your gold in the ground. See, here is what belongs to you."

His master replied, "You wicked, lazy servant! So you knew that I harvest where I have not sown and gather where I have not scattered seed? Well then, you should have put my money on deposit with the bankers, so that when I returned I would have received it back with interest.

"Take the bag of gold from him and give it to the one who has ten bags. For those who have will be given more, and they will have an abundance. As for those who do not have, even what they have will be taken from them. And throw that worthless servant outside, into the darkness, where there will be weeping and gnashing of teeth."

The coins, even the metaphoric ones you hold as you read this story, grow a bit heavier as the story goes on, don't they? The master gave two responses to the servants for the way they approached the task they were given: "Well done, good and faithful servant" or "You wicked lazy servant." Yes, the context for the Matthew passage is predominantly about the Kingdom of Heaven; however, the story has plenty to offer us as well.

You might wonder if God is going away and won't check back in with you until either you're on the field or you and all

A Bowl of Coins

your bags are back on your home turf. Feel the coins in your hand. This transition is going to happen. Unlike the master in the story, God is not simply going to go off on a journey, only to return in the end. He will be with you every step of the way. At times his presence will be obvious, but there will be times when you will wonder if he has gone off on his own.

Regardless of your feelings, God is with you and in the not-too-distant future the new job or assignment will be a reality, the boxes will be unpacked, and the children will be in a new school setting. You will either invest the time well or you won't. It's that simple and that complicated. I say complicated because if finishing well was a given, you wouldn't need this book. As you look back, I want you to hear, "You finished well, your relationships remain in intact, your finances are in order, you have kept love the heartbeat of your interactions, you have handed off the baton to those following you, and your emotional reactions have been managed in a way that leaves you proud. Well done, good and faithful servant."

Accepting the tension of this season

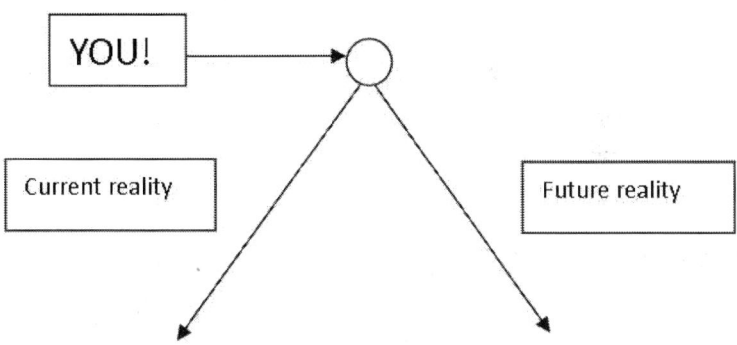

Right now you are living with the tension captured in this illustration. The left side is your current situation and on the right the new situation you will be in. Both sides may be attrac-

Looming Transitions

tive, but at present you do not fully belong on either side, and it is exhausting to live with the tension. To relieve the tension, the ball wants to pick one side or the other, and roll toward it. I bet you can relate. It gets old and tiring to have to live moment by moment, day by day, especially when it drags into month by month with this tension. But that is what you are being asked to do. Clearly, this illustration oversimplifies reality. Yet I have found this image helpful in the months leading up to leaving for the field or from it. When you feel like your identity, roles, and finances are being poked, remind yourself, although unpleasant, this is a normal part of a looming transition. The day will come when the transition will be in the rearview mirror, and you will be rooted.

Keeping your soul fertile

I shared earlier that part of my journey involves a three-year study leave from the field, even though I was still on full-time support and worked in China each summer. The plan was to complete a two-year M.A. in counseling and during the third year work on the licensing process. That had been the plan, and I won't get bogged down here with what really happened; after two years I did graduate and wrote the following in a newsletter to supporters.

It is hard to believe it, but I graduated last Saturday and am at another transition point. This semester I read a book by Donald Miller called *Through Painted Deserts* in which he wrote about a road trip from Austin, Texas, to Portland, Oregon. This road trip is analogous to many life journeys because Don had to leave what was familiar to travel with someone he didn't know well. It was in the traveling that he got to know his companion and see different sides of himself and the Creator. In the prologue he wrote:

All my life I have been changing . . . Everybody has to

A Bowl of Coins

change, or they expire. Everybody has to leave, everybody has to leave home and come back so they can love it again for all new reasons. I want to keep my soul fertile for the changes, so things keep getting born in me, so things keep dying when it is time for things to die. I want to keep walking away from the person I was a moment ago, because a mind was made to figure things out, not to read the same page recurrently.[5]

I was challenged by this idea of keeping my soul fertile *so that* things can be born in me and die when it is time for them to die. Even though life is full of transitions, I am not all that keen on going through them. This semester as I lived in the reality that I would graduate and have to say goodbye to another phase of life, a routine I enjoy and people who have become dear to me, I thought about this idea of letting things die when it is time for them to die.

One of my professors retired at the end of this semester, and frankly speaking, he "died" a semester ago. His body was in the classroom, but his mind and energy had moved on to what he was going to do after he retired. He was more than just a professor, he was also my spiritual formation leader, and his "absence," both emotionally and physically, irritated me. Reading Donald Miller's quote, watching this truly beloved professor, and knowing my own dislike of having to say goodbye, AGAIN? I thought about how hard it is to live with the tension of not dying too early or holding on too long. I didn't come to any easy answers, but that is a bit of what I have been thinking about recently as school has died and the phase of being a licensed counselor begins. Thanks for your continued love, prayers, and support. I'm blessed and grateful,
Amy

I imagine this resonates with you as well, this idea of keeping your soul fertile. Even though I read many books in seminary, it is this passage from a book I wasn't required to read that echoes on. I want a fertile soul. I want to be the kind of person who is able to let roles or locations or seasons of life die so there is space for the new to grow.

You're on this journey too or you probably wouldn't be reading this. When a transition is looming, part of keeping your soul fertile is awareness. Awareness of the kind of person you want to be. Awareness that it is possible to let certain parts die and plant new ones. Awareness that fertile can look fallow on the surface. Awareness that it is hard to let parts of yourself die, but it is necessary. Awareness that you may need to leave to stay you. Awareness that while a fertile soul may not be the heart cry of the world, it is the heart cry of God. He loves you and cares more about being *with* you in this journey than *where* you are going.

This process of dying might be easier if you are moving toward a role or season that excites you. If this is not a wanted transition you don't have to pretend it is, but you do need to guard against seeds of bitterness being sown. We will talk more about grief later, so if you're left with questions, make a note of them and we will get to them.

When it doesn't go well

While keeping your soul fertile is admirable, that doesn't mean it is easy. Remember the ball, sitting atop the point? How do you "die" at the right time without letting that ball prematurely go to one side or the other to relieve the tension? With any transition there are going to be bumps and the goal isn't to get it just right—we'll touch more on that in Chapter Five. Because if that is your goal, chances are you will fail and fail miserably. So as much as you, your spouse, your kids, your friends, and strangers you interact with along the way might want you to get it right, let that one go.

It is understandable to want to relieve the tension present in a looming change, and little releases, such as checking out by watching a T.V. show or ignoring a big decision for part of the day, are normal and helpful. This is normal, temporary dying.

A Bowl of Coins

Although dying on the small scale creates pressure valves in life, dying too soon or too late on a larger scale can create long lasting messes. How does dying poorly play out in real life?

Tension relieved by staying in the current reality: raptured apartment

Remember Sally from the beginning of the chapter? She had known that she'd be moving and leaving China for at least half a year. She had time to sort through her possessions, give some away, and throw others out. Sally was a bit of a collector, so this was going to be no small task. She'd been in China for years, and this was an earthquake of a move for her, disrupting everything in her life. Everything. As she came up to it, she was probably overwhelmed by her life changing so radically. She relieved the tension by rolling toward her China life, and giving me a taste of what the rapture might look like if I was left behind.

Herein lies the rub of dying too late: as with a boat speeding by, others have to live in the wake you create. It doesn't matter how much you do not intend or desire to leave a wake, you will leave one. The question becomes, what kind of wake will you leave? One that knocks other people over or one that jostles without upending? In the raptured apartment, you could say it was fairly limited as only one person was, shall we say, sloshed with water from Sally's wake.

But that is not always the case; sometimes the mess involves many. I received the following email from a friend about a sticky situation she stepped into, inheriting a mess by someone who didn't have enough regard for those who followed:

> Dear Amy,
> I just thought I would share with you a bit of a tale from the dark side, so grab a spot of black tea.
> Well, things have gone along swimmingly here until today when Jake asked if I could help with a little cleanup of the 2nd floor apartment since the school had a Japanese

Looming Transitions

teacher set to move in at 5pm. So, three of us went down to help Mrs. Liu, our caretaker, ready the apartment. Our job was just to remove the stuff we wanted and decide what was trash.

Amy, Amy, Amy . . . I know you have heard horror stories before about what people find in apartments, but this one was unlike any I have ever seen. Let's see . . . what was the worst part?

The "Lady Care" products strewn all over the place? (Poor Bill) The personal financial information the teacher left behind?The private work information she left? The sensitive materials she left? (Including her diaries?) The gifts and pictures of students? (How hurtful if word gets out!)The sofa covers that were left in the washing machine, clean. But now a crumpled mess? (They belong to the school.)

No, by far it had to be the three potatoes we found on her bed hidden under a bunch of covers. One of the potatoes was peeled, all were incredibly rotten. Along with them were some mustard, ketchup, mayo, and a package of opened butter.

I apologized profusely to Mrs. Liu for the overall condition of the apartment, but when we hit the potatoes (she found the first two and I found the peeled one), and other stash of stuff—all having sullied the bed—I was speechless; that is, after I screamed upon my discovery of them.

Whatever the "good news" work that she did in her years here, I celebrate, but I must say that the mess she left here is one that will not be forgotten by the school. What she did can be forgiven by the team, but she missed an opportunity to bless the George family and the entire team by eliminating this ordeal of hours spent cleaning up after her.

Mrs. Liu and I had a lovely chat Saturday about issues dear to her heart. I feel now like we have disappointed her before we really have even gotten to start a relation-

A Bowl of Coins

ship. I am not about to lose hope, though. I know even this situation can be redeemed. Am I being really Chinese in wishing that the teacher would write a self-criticism and send it to the school?

My hope is that this disgusting thing never ever happens again in China.

Much love to you!

What in heaven's name were three potatoes doing in the bed? And one of them peeled? Seriously? Opened butter in the bed? Raptured doesn't even begin to describe it. Who peels a potato, sticks it at the foot of the bed, and then forgets it? It's tempting to think it was a self-absorbed jerk being clueless. It wasn't. This was a kind, thoughtful young woman I would gladly have teamed with. So, lest you (or I) think this could not happen to us, we need to remember she was simply someone who relieved the tension of living with one foot in the current reality and the other in the future reality in a way that was out of character.

Her future reality came, and she left. But not without creating a wake that impacted her former employer and colleagues far beyond what she intended or ever imagined. As you can guess, it took more time and effort to restore relationships than it took to tear holes in them.

Tension relieved by moving on to the future reality: empty apartment

Of course, there is the other side of the model: people who relieve the tension of the here-and-now by mentally leaving long before their bodies join them.

A good eight months before my friend Kelly moved to another city, she started going through her cupboards and putting together packages for her friends. Some days I'd wake to find a grocery bag full of goodies hanging from my front door and a note saying, "I thought you'd like all of my coconut and some muffin liners." Or another friend would come home to discover that a bag full of popcorn kernels, taco seasoning, and other spices had been hung on her door during the day. Part of it was exacerbated by the fact that Kelly's job wound down considerably before it was time for her to move. I wish this was uncommon prior to leaving for the field or from it. Sadly people tend to be either extremely busy or extremely bored.

Two to three months before she moved, she had sold or given away basically everything. It was more than cooking supplies; her walls were blank, her shelves were empty, and front and center in her living room were her half-packed suitcases. For two months. Visiting her home before she left was more like visiting a squatter who happened to have a couch. And two suitcases. Kelly's wake might not be as obvious, but it's there. In her case, people stopped dropping by and visiting her at home. They wanted to spend time with her, yet sitting in her living room, it was clear that she wasn't really a part of our world anymore. She had moved on but had the unfortunate situation of needing to kill about seventy days.

Or take Sarah. She met Brian when they both worked in China. He had returned to the U.S., and then they started dating. Sarah had seven months left on her contract, but wanted to be released from it so she could be near her boyfriend. It's understandable to want to be near a new love (who did turn out to be her husband). Yet when the organization said she needed to stay to the end of her commitment, she shared her displeasure on a regular basis.

At the time war was imminent in the Middle East and a hot topic of discussion was whether or not it might require us to be evacuated. Sarah's mom encouraged Sarah that God may be answering her prayers to be with Brian through the (potential) evacuation. This was not a onetime random comment. Sarah passed on this "word of hope" to us. To relieve the tension Sarah and her mom seemed to welcome the idea of a war over Sarah staying in China to fulfill her obligation.

Thankfully war didn't break out. Her body stayed in her job, but you can guess where Sarah's heart and interests lay as she

A Bowl of Coins

spent days buying things for her wedding—even though she wasn't engaged. As we helped load her many suitcases into the cab headed for the airport, it was with a sense of relief that Sarah and the stink of her early death would be gone.[6]

The irony is not lost on me that the majority of examples are from someone's living space. In general, the home is often a more accurate expression of what's going on for a person than external settings, such as an office or school. Tension exists because indeed there *does* need to be a death to the current reality, and life cannot go on the same. The tension also exists because no two situations are the same, thus removing simple or easy answers. And that is the primary way to know if you are living with the tension. *Is it there? Do you sense the tension?*

When my sister was put on Prednisone for pneumonia, she was warned that one of the side effects is hunger and often weight gain. She was told, "Learn to live with hunger." Not exactly the message our culture sends. But isn't that a rich paradox: she still needed to eat to stay alive, yet she also had to learn to befriend this unwelcome new companion, hunger.

So we return to the question, do you sense tension? If so, learn to live with it for this season. The tension itself, if you let it, can become a sign that you haven't died too early or too late. It could be that you are relieving the tension in healthy ways (e.g., having lunch with a friend, getting things done on your to-do list). If the tension isn't there, ask yourself why. The absence of tension over a prolonged time could be a warning sign to you that you are finding unhealthy ways to die either too late or too soon, leaving a wake you didn't intend.

After editing this chapter, my editor returned to this point and commented, "You don't include any positive examples of people living with the tension and finishing well. Is it possible?" Hope exists! Liz had served in Southeast Asia and relocated to the home office of our organization. One summer when I stopped by her department to say hi to everyone, she thanked me for the workshop. In her unsolicited feedback she said her transition from the field had been the smoothest transition she'd made and it was because she had a plan, expected it to be messy, and made time for what was important to her. She concluded by saying that finishing well helped her be ready for the next phase. I had stopped by to say hi, but I left encouraged. You do not have to be a cautionary tale.

Cultivating fertility

The concept of fertility and bearing new life is found primarily in two arenas: agriculture and pregnancy. Both have become billion-dollar industries in the U.S. with considerable effort, technology, and manpower poured into them. Literally blood, sweat, and tears. Why? Because fertility isn't a given. Just ask the couple who have spent hours waiting in doctors' offices and have had more invasive procedures than they'd care to remember. Infertile couples have become armchair experts in ovulation, sperm counts, and motility as they chart with scientific precision temperatures and times. Hoping *this* will be the month they don't experience yet another small death. Yet hope is dashed once again. Why? Because fertility isn't a given.

Keeping your soul fertile is hard work. But there are areas where a difference can be made in how fertile a field is. One of the reasons that farming and gardening are rewarding is because there is a clear product, one that can be seen, touched, and monitored. While keeping your soul fertile will not be as tangible, there will still be aspects that can be seen, touched, and monitored. You will leave a wake; this is a part of life. The question is will it be one in which you have indeed finished well, or will it slosh those around you needlessly?

Chapter Two

The Stress of Endings

Farming looks mighty easy when your plow is a pencil and you're a thousand miles from the corn field.
— Dwight D. Eisenhower

Kermit was right: it's not easy being green.[7] My first cross-cultural experience began in my own country with a six-hundred-mile move. This Colorado girl chose to attend the great and wonderful University of Kansas. As the firstborn, what for me was an exciting next step in life was gut-wrenching for my mom. With three children born one year apart, I was the first from her brood to leave and a reminder that all too soon the job she loved would be coming to an end — or at least changing significantly — whether she wanted it to or not. This was before the days of cheap long distance plans or cell phones. I don't recall talking that often, but when the first phone bill arrived, Dad was shocked at the amount and must have commented about it to my mom.

Always quick on her feet, she replied, "I miss my child and you can pay for the phone bill or you can pay for me to go to counseling. Frankly I don't care which you choose." The phone bill looked like a pretty good deal. As the story was retold years later, it embodied a life lesson for me. The question isn't if you will pay; instead the question really is *how* will you choose to spend and invest your resources? The spending can take many different forms — time, effort, relationships, or money.

A common activity used when people prepare to go to the field or debrief from a term involves using blue and yellow play

Looming Transitions

dough. Yellow represents your home culture and blue your host culture. Once you have gone to the field, you'll never be completely yellow again because parts of you will change. But you'll also never transition completely to blue and be an insider to your host culture. When you hear of my love for the Denver Broncos (American football), my desire to have variety in my diet, and that I drive on the right side of the road, that's my yellowness coming through. The blue land I lived in watched Ping-Pong for hours, wanted rice or noodles at almost every meal, and crossed the street when there was a break in traffic. I'm green because many of the Super Bowls I've watched had Thai drink commercials, rice once a day is often enough, and, sadly, I get annoyed with drivers in both countries. Now I'm part yellow, part blue, and a growing bit of green.

How did the yellow and blue become green in the play dough illustration? By being mashed together. Time and effort combined with intention. As you are getting ready to move, whether from yellow to blue or blue to yellow, it would be nice if one phase of life ended without heartache and the next phase fell effortlessly into place. No squashing. No bumps and bruising. No stress.

It *almost* goes without saying that when something comes to an end there is going to be stress. Because it seems so obvious, we tend to forget to acknowledge the impact of stress on our thoughts, feelings, souls, reactions, and even our bodies as we report with a cursory "Stressful!" when asked "How's it going?" In the midst of my own major transition, even I didn't realize how stressed I was until I was no longer smack dab in the middle of it. I invite you to be kind to yourself during this season. Acknowledging stress is not the same as elevating it; stress should not become a free pass for bad behavior, laziness, or rudeness. Just because you are preparing for a time of change doesn't give you a "today is a free day to be a jerk" card. But it is important to recognize effects of stress and have a game plan in advance.

Up to now, we've been using the word "stress" casually without clarifying the term. It will be helpful to define stress so

The Stress of Endings

that we can see the role it plays in looming tran[sitions so that] it can hinder our best endeavors.

Stress: the problem is in the gaps

While both good and bad get lumped in together under the label stress, technically the good is called *eustress* and the bad *distress*. Getting married is not the same as being told you have cancer, but both will add stress to life. Regardless of whether an event brings eustress or distress, the reason it is stressful and the impacts are similar. The following definition from Doc Childre and Howard Martin provides insight:

> Stress is the body and mind's response to any stressful pressure that disrupts the balance in the mind or body. It occurs when our *perceptions* of events don't meet our *expectations* and we don't manage our reaction to the *disappointment*. As a *response*, stress expresses itself as resistance, tension, strain or frustration, that throws off our physiological and psychological equilibrium, keeping us out-of-sync and stressed-out.[8] *(Italics added)*

Expectations. Perceptions. Disappointment. Response. If you can remember those four words over the next few months, they will help make sense of the stress you are experiencing. Stress often starts with a gap between our expectation and perception. If you come home late from work and expect your spouse to be annoyed because you didn't call and indeed they are annoyed, the perception and expectation aren't that far off. While it's stressful, it's not as stressful as when you arrive home thinking that you've got a quiet evening in front of you (expectation) and the reality when you check your messages is that you need to complete an important document needed to process your visa within the next three hours (perception of reality). Now, if you

Looming Transitions

that the form would be coming sometime in the next several days, your level of disappointment isn't surprisingly high. However, if you thought all of your paperwork was done, the disappointment often fuels a harsher response.

It's often not your child, the post office worker, the late bill, or the visa paperwork that's the problem; the root is the gap between hope (expectation) and reality (perception), resulting in a response landing somewhere on the disappointment continuum. Most of us know this, but in the moment where expectations and perceptions clash, it's simpler to blame the child or the postal worker, isn't it? Anything but yourself. If it is "out there" then it's not your fault, and you are freed up to complain and fuss. When it comes to life's transitions, you need to be responsible for your own patterns of handling stress. Monitoring and managing stress will be necessary in the next few months.

Responses to Stress

Having responses to stress isn't the core problem; it's the responses themselves that dictate how well you are managing stress during transition. And responses often point to expectations. Part of finishing well is being aware of your own expectations. While it might be nice to think that you will regularly check in with yourself about the expectations you have about work, relationships, or God, the truth is you probably don't. However, because transitions require facing something that has the potential to be a field of land mines, it is worth the time and effort to think through some of the big categories before beginning the journey.

Before we look at setting realistic expectations, let's pause and explore the areas when it comes to large moves in which unrealistic expectations may be lurking:

- **Time frame**: How long will fund-raising, processing visas, or packing take?
- **Finances**: How much will the move cost, and what are

you willing to spend? (e.g., will you move yourself or hire movers?)
- **Roles**: Who will do what? (otherwise known as "I thought *you* were doing that!")
- **Storage**: Will storing possessions be involved? How much needs to be gotten rid of before the transition?
- **Housing**: Will you need to stay with others as your departure date nears?
- **Activities**: What activities do you want to be sure to do or places you want visit one last time?
- **Counsel**: Whom do you need to talk to about these expectations and the stress you're feeling? This could involve formal or informal counseling.
- **Paperwork**: What paperwork will be involved in this transition?

Not all of these areas will be of the same value or importance, and each transition is different. However, most of the areas will be touched by expectations. It's also helpful to remember that setting expectations is not a "one and done" process.

If only this were as easy as setting a table

It's not like you can start from an empty table and neatly set your expectations like plates and silverware in an orderly fashion. We all already have expectations about the process and where we are going. When I first moved to China, I had no sense (another way of saying I had rather unrealistic expectations) of what would really fit into my two large suitcases. I expected that all I planned to take would fit. So when it didn't, I was a basket case. You don't want to be dealing with avoidable problems the night before you are to board a big plane with all your worldly possessions. I had expectations about my luggage; I didn't set them very well, however. That's why we want to talk about this now—it's a more neutral time than when you're in the thick of it and freak-out mode is your only option.

Setting realistic expectations helps to clarify the items on the list above. Setting also provides you a benchmark from which to monitor both the completion of a task and how realistic a plan is once it's set into motion.[9] We've all made plans we need to modify. If you've planned ahead, you have more wiggle room. You might wonder why so much space is given to expectations; it is because unrealistic expectations are the primary contributors to our stress. The more you are able to "benchmark and monitor" your expectations, the more you will be able to respond to people and situations in ways that leave you proud of yourself at the end of this transition.[10] Take a moment and list an expectation you have in regards to each area. For example, "In regards to time, I expect ..." This list will become your benchmark starting point.

Major life transitions, and those nearest to us

Stress will show cracks in the relationships, exposing issues. Some you are aware of, but others may surprise you. My teammate Jess liked to get things checked off her to-do list and with a large family, the list was pretty long. Steve, her husband, was the kind of person who wanted to do a task 100% or not at all. When it came to packing up their books, he wanted to take the time to review each book instead of making quick decision whether to store, ship, or give away. Jess and Steve knew this about themselves and each other. What surprised them as they packed to move back to the U.S. was that they expected each other to behave differently turning the transition. Jess thought Steve would make faster decisions because of the amount of tasks to be done. Steve expected Jess to complete a job to perfection since they didn't want to have to redo the sorting once they arrived in the U.S. Now, this is not a major issue or even one that surprised Steve and Jess. What did surprise them was this was not their first transition (or even their second or third), and yet they expected each other to change.

Hidden expectations are common and can be addressed. One

way to know if hidden expectations are occurring between you and someone else is to look for SWAT signs.[11]

- **Scorekeeping**: when one or both of you are keeping track of who does what.
- **Wheel Spinning**: when you talk about the same problem over and over again. When an argument starts with you thinking, "Here we go again."
- **Avoidance**: when one or both of you are avoiding certain topics or levels of intimacy.
- **Trivial Triggers**: when trivial issues are blown up out of all proportion. A small event triggers horrendous arguments.

You can see how any of the above could play out between Steve and Jess. If you notice one or more of the above in yourself, it is helpful to rank the problem on a scale of 1-10 with one being fairly benign and ten being the breaking point of the relationship. For areas that are less severe, weigh how much this needs to be addressed now. Can it wait until you've moved? For those that are more severe, seeking professional help in the midst of the transition may help to save a relationship.

What causes stress?

Though unrealistic expectations are a primary contributor to stress, they aren't the only cause. Dr. Archibald Hart answers the question "What causes stress?" with the following list.[12] Stress may result from anything that:

- Annoys
- Threatens
- Prods
- Excites
- Scares
- Worries

Looming Transitions

- Hurries
- Angers
- Frustrates
- Challenges
- Criticizes or
- Reduces your self esteem

I think I heard you laugh as you read going, "Check, got that one. Check, got that one too!" In keeping your soul fertile and prepared for a transition, there is simply no way to avoid parts of the experience being threatening or exciting or challenging. And people are going to have opinions on the way you make decisions or make comments that might have more of a critical tone than you'd like. It comes as no surprise that this will be a stressful time; but often we don't realize the cumulative stress assault we'll face when we prepare to relocate to another culture. Hopefully this list normalizes the scope and magnitude of what you're going through. You're normal.

I've also seen people feed their stress and instead of normalizing and acknowledging it, they grow it. Are you concerned about your child having friends? Then you're a normal parent. Are you consumed by it? If so, it could be you've displaced other areas you're worried about into this one and nursed it out of proportion. Regardless of the reason, the biggest way to help shrink over-grown stressors is to tell a friend or group. There is power in bringing these stressors to light and not bearing them alone. You can also involve people in tending to your stress by asking them to pray about specific concerns. When people ask how they can pray for you, hand them a list of the causes of stress (Anything that "annoys, threatens, prods ...") and ask them to pray through the list as you come to mind.

We have been designed by God to bear an incredible amount of stress as long as we build in recovery time. Sabbath itself is built on the principle of worship and rest. The problem is that many of us ignore warning symptoms of stress by either becoming addicted to adrenaline or turning a blind eye until permanent damage occurs.

The Stress of Endings

We can become like the proverbial frog in the kettle that doesn't notice the heat until it is too late. Each person responds to stress uniquely. Some will be more prone to physical effects while others will experience more emotional ones. One person's body will experience a variety of the symptoms, while other's bodies just one or two but experience them to an extreme degree. And to add to the fun, the stressful situation doesn't just happen to one person; it impacts an entire system of people and often multiple systems at once. Your marriage, family, friends, social groups, possibly people at work, and your stress in one way or another will affect church.

No, your tooth doesn't need to be pulled

You may already be aware of the different ways in which your body takes in and expresses stress. I know life is more stressful than normal when I have pain in my jaw from clenching it. Years ago, I had a tooth that needed to come out. When I walked in to the appointment, I told them we could save a bunch of time because I knew I had a tooth that needed to come out. I pointed to the tooth. With a twinkle in his eye, my new dentist calmly explained that wasn't how they did dentistry and he would do all they could to preserve the tooth. Well, the pain was off the chart. I knew it needed to come out, but since I needed his help in removing it, I went along with his little "save a tooth" plan.

Imagine my shock when he showed me the X-ray of my healthy tooth. What?! Why was the pain at a ridiculous level? He explained I was under so much stress during the day my body was processing it by grinding and clenching as I slept. He said I was grinding my teeth so aggressively that, without intervention, I was on the path to have nubs for teeth. Charming picture. I've slept with a mouth guard ever since and learned that my jaw is one of the ways my body warns about stress. Our bodies are beautiful and complex systems, leading to an array of assault locations for stress. Here are some of the physical effects of stress:[13]

- Increased heart rate

Looming Transitions

- Increased blood pressure
- Rapid breathing
- Muscles will tense
- Hands will get cool and clammy
- Digestion is reduced
- Instincts in brain will override the system which decreases ability to think clearly
- Sensitivity to noises is enhanced
- Lowered libido
- Head, back, and neck aches
- High blood pressure
- Panic and/or anxiety
- Stomach problems
- Auto-immune problems like allergies or some forms of arthritis
- Sleeping problems
- TMJ

Do you know how your body processes stress? When you think back over previous life transitions you've experienced, which of these have occurred. Pause to reflect on when you went to college, or moved to a new city, or moved to a new country. If I find myself wide-awake in the middle of the night and my stomach in knots, I know my stress is off the charts. For me, this is the emergency system of body wailing the siren that I am nearing a very dangerous place. Because they are rare, I have learned to heed these warnings. What are the signs you're under an alarming amount of stress? Where do your warning sirens sound?

I got the stomach flu two days before I left for pre-field orientation when I moved full time to the field. The timing seemed odd as we'd been having an enjoyable family time in the mountains and had returned to Denver. Nobody else in my family was sick, so it wasn't something I'd eaten or a bug we were sharing. Looking back, I can see this was my body manifesting the truth. Even though I was eagerly anticipating meeting my teammate in person and starting our life overseas, I was about to walk away from every person I knew. I was leaving the familiar for the unfamiliar. As if to hammer another nail in my mom's heart, I left on her birthday. While such poetic coincidences are charming in novels and movies, they are cruel in real life.

My parents wanted to come and wait with me in the boarding area, which was still a possibility then. I already felt guilty leaving my parents on Mom's birthday, but I could not imagine how awkward it would be to chit-chat early in the morning and then sob in front of strangers when the time came for our first big goodbye. I told them I couldn't do it; we needed to rip the bandage off outside the airport. I knew they were annoyed with me (we're not the only ones with emotions all over the board), but in the end agreed to drop me off.

Physical reactions are not the only ones; you'll have emotional ones too

The following list includes some of the emotional reactions that can occur from stressful situations:[14]

- Lack of attachment
- Dramatic swings in emotion
- Never feeling settled
- Sense of feeling different
- Thinking other peoples' lives are more meaningful
- Irritability
- Cloudy thinking
- Obsessive thinking
- Feeling distant from God
- Guilt

Feel better after reading through the list? Probably yes and no. If you experience any—hopefully not all—of the above, know that you are normal. Over the years, I've noticed in the days leading up to returning to the field, the people around me increasingly annoy me. While I'd like to blame them and say they really are that annoying, the truth is, it's hard to say goodbye. I make it more bearable by unconsciously detaching and becoming annoyed.

What's your precious?

In *The Lord of the Rings,* Gollum is known for stroking the ring and calling it "my precious, my precious" in a creepy and distressed whisper. We can be like that with the ways our bodies and emotions respond to stress. You have a pet approach or two among your responses to stress. Maybe a stomachache is your "precious," or your neck muscles become really tight. On the emotional front you might find yourself detaching or becoming unusually forgetful. Ironically what can make stress so stressful in times of transition is that the way our bodies respond can be unpredictable. Be on the lookout for both familiar ways of dealing with stress as well as a few newcomers. I wish I could tell you that you will have at least one unexpected way of coping. Or that if this is your *third* move you will feel a certain, predictable way. But each time that we go through a big change can bring predictable patterns from our history as well as curveballs.

No man is an island

No man is an island, entire of itself; every man is a piece of the continent, a part of the main; if a clod be washed away by the sea, Europe is the less . . . any man's death diminishes me, because I am involved in mankind.
–John Donne[15]

John Donne's famous poem is well known because it captures truth succinctly, creating a visual picture of the relational webs we are a part of. A modern image of these relational webs is a baby mobile. Hanging over the baby's crib, a mobile is made up of distinct pieces, maybe barn animals or shapes or something

The Stress of Endings

else pleasing to a child's eye. Each object dangles alone, but if the infant reaches out and tugs on the pig it isn't only the pig that gets jiggled. Every one of the animals will move a bit.

Although our relational webs are less tangible than the strings on a mobile, they are no less real. When you are stressed, it is not just you who is jostled. True, it may be *your* head that hurts or back that is tense or sleep that is disturbed. But others feel the looming transition too. When I was returning to the U.S. for a study leave, on more than one occasion my parents said they'd understand if I wanted to get my own apartment. I thought they were just being polite. After living in a country where a small village could fit in their house, being on full-time support, and knowing the cost of living in the U.S. was high, I couldn't imagine not living with them. It turns out those kind comments were indirect expressions of them being impacted by my decisions.

Your stressful situations are going to be picked up, felt and even shared by others. As mentioned earlier, that doesn't give you (or them) a free pass to behave poorly. You will need to find ways to process stress without creating needless distance between you and others. And when your words or actions are harsher, sharper or stronger than intended, be quick to own it. Go to the people impacted and, depending on whether you merely behaved badly or you outright sinned against them, proceed accordingly. Earlier we talked about the effects of stress. Here I'm referring to when you have crossed a line. I'll admit it's hard to own when you've been a jerk. To make it easier, it might help to explain you've been reading this book and are more aware of the effects of stress. One of the effects is in how you respond to people or situations. If you have crossed a line and need to apologize, a simple but effective formula to follow involves three parts:

1. Briefly state what you did
2. Describe how you think it impacted the other person
3. Ask for forgiveness

If you begin to fall into patterns and find yourself needing to apologize repeatedly for similar types of offenses, you may need to add two more steps:

4. Describe why you're interested in changing the offensive behavior
5. Describe a self-imposed penalty for not changing

Because transition often involves multiple people at once, you might also need to help others' children process through the stress they are under and the ways they experience it physically and emotionally. After talking with your kids about stress and how they process it, follow up conversations could look like this:

- Remember how we talked about stress affecting our bodies and feelings? Do you think some of Sally's not sharing with you is her way of showing she's stressed?
- Wow, Steve doesn't usually punch people! I wonder if that's one of the ways he's showing you how much he's going to miss you?
- I'm sorry your stomach hurts. It's not fun being in pain and sometimes it helps to understand where the pain comes from. Do you think your stomach is telling you something about your stress? On a scale of 1 to 10 where one is no stress and 10 is totally stressed, where would you put yourself right now? This week?

While it would be nice to shield our children from stress, one of the most helpful gifts we can give them are the tools they will need to handle stress in life. Normalizing reactions to stress helps children make sense of what's going on.

Don't be surprised if all your reactions aren't super holy

I surprised myself.

About two weeks before, I'd finished packing up my life, selling, shipping, or throwing out my earthly possessions, and

The Stress of Endings

boarded a plane back to the U.S. without a plan as to what was next. I had ideas and hopes, but no real plan. I'd left my favorite apartment (the bookshelves alone were a reason to stay on the field), the one where I felt all grown up in. I left a vibrant community I loved. I left a job I was good at. I left a sweet neighborhood with convenient shopping, great Chinese food, and a life-giving gym. I also left organization politics and a job that seemed to be shrinking in on me.

My friend Lisa called—only two hours time difference instead of on opposite sides of the same day!—wondering how I was doing. We started off as colleagues and teammates in Beijing and had become lifelong friends so I didn't need to give her the sanitized version; she knew the good, the bad, and the ugly about my story.

Without missing a beat, *Relieved*, popped out.

What? Wasn't the "right" answer supposed to be sad or excited? Wasn't I sad that in order to move forward with what God had next for me required so much effort, money? Wasn't I excited to see what was around the next bend in life? Truthfully? No. The sadness (and anger) would come, as would the excitement, but in that moment, on the couch, I was awash in relief. I had been leading workshops on finishing well and had even written the rough draft of this book. I don't remember *relief* being one of the fruits of the spirit. I had finished well, so shouldn't I have had a more spiritual reaction like joy or peace? This is the nature of stress. It's going to happen, and transitioning from one culture to another carries additional stresses because you won't fully fit in anywhere.

The splendor of fall's color: people are like leaves

Part of the beauty of leaves turning yellow and orange and red in the fall is that they do not all turn at the exact same time. They also don't all turn the exact same colors. We are compelled to comment every fall, aren't we? What's beautiful in nature can be annoying when something similar happens in our own lives.

Looming Transitions

Even though the trees are transitioning from one season to another and we like the variety of colors, we may not like it when others around us are changing at different rates. To return to the play dough example from the beginning of the chapter, while it seems obvious that not everyone will turn green to the same extent or in the same way from those yellow and blue balls of dough getting mashed together, somehow we expect sameness. But as we've learned, unrealistic expectations will lead to disappointment and even more stress.

This chapter started with Kermit's well-known song in which he sang about the travails of being green. He sang about facing life the color of a leaf and the challenge of blending in. At this point in the journey, pay attention to your expectations and the gaps that occur between them and your perceptions. As much as you monitor them and try to minimize them, the gaps will still be there. Be kind to yourself and others as you become green or another shade of green, knowing that you will experience both physical and emotional responses. You're not losing your mind. Your family members haven't been replaced with evil aliens. You're simply becoming green.

We've looked at three givens: (1) you're going to leave a wake, (2) you're going to be stressed, and (3) you will have expectations. The rest of this book will be dedicated to helping you process and approach the seven areas mentioned in the introduction:

- Stay Grounded in Christ
- Laughter Revives the Soul
- Accept That It's Going to Be Messy
- Know Yourself
- Start Early
- It's Not Just About You
- Work Out Your Grief

As you prepare for the next chapter, does it surprise you to find out I don't think quiet times with God are necessary when you transition?

Chapter 3

Stay Grounded in Christ

The LORD will guide you always; He will satisfy your needs in a sun-scorched land and will strengthen your frame. You will be like a well-watered garden, like a spring whose water never fails.
—Isaiah 58:11

"I want you to know, the Hillyard family will miss you," my friend and colleague Dan said out of the side of his mouth. We were at an annual Christmas decorating party for coworkers and their family members. Thankfully we were surrounded by chaotic energy and noise. In that moment it felt like we were in the eye of a storm. Those around us could hear every word said, but I knew others were unaware the floor had just opened up and swallowed me whole.

It was Friday night, and I had until Sunday night to declare my official intentions for the next year. Since my job, although fairly constant for nearly ten years, had morphed over the years, this wasn't normally a big deal. But as happens to all of us at some point, this time was different. I had decided in August this would be my last year with my organization and had sat on the news until it was time to go public. As the day drew closer, a few close friends were brought in on the news, yet I knew it wasn't appropriate to say anything more broadly until my boss knew. So when Dan said, "I want you to know, the Hillyard family will miss you," I took a small step back as the tears got to my eyes faster than my brain processed what he had said. I must have looked sucker-punched because Dan, a non-hugger, put his arm around me. So much for pretending this phase of my life was going to go on. I could sense the impact this change would have on my soul.

God is the same yesterday, today, and tomorrow, but in that moment at the Christmas party, I entered another season of finishing well. God is the same, yes. I, however, would never be the same once this piece of me moved from the shadows of my heart to the open reality of my life.

You know what I mean. You know that you will be altered by this transition, whether to or from the field. This is not a value statement, but a fact. Even though this is a season of being uprooted and replanting, you can stay grounded in the One who never changes. The One who knew and loved you from one end of eternity to the other. As you change, he's inviting you to wander with him on new paths.

Will the anchor hold?

In the upcoming months, as you transition from one locale to another, there will be times when God meets you in amazing ways and provides for you in tender moments. However, there might be severe disappointments and frustrations as doors you thought were open slam shut, support doesn't come through, plans fall apart, and slices of dreams are shattered in inexplicable ways. As you are on the cusp of your transition, preparing to dive in, I don't want to be presumptuous about the ways God is going to work. But I have confidence in saying that you will be marked by this transition.

Fertile souls and fertile fields are similar in holding broader stories, not just one transition or crop. The story a farmer will tell about a field often incorporates years and sometimes decades of crops. "Remember back in the summer of '99 when we almost didn't make it?" "The heat this year is nothing like it was last year!" "I wonder what the price of corn will be next year." It's not simply about what is happening right now. There is an eye on the past as *this* crop becomes a part of the history of the field

Stay Grounded in Christ

and another eye to the future and the hope of other crops that will be planted. Fertility for that field holds the past, present, and future together. It is both about this one crop and about all of the crops before and after.

Likewise with the soul. This transition before you *is* significant in and of itself, and parts of you, your family, and your story will forever be altered because of it. And yet, it is about more than this one event, as it joins a larger story. This transition will not become the sum of your life. However, that doesn't preclude it from being a significant marker that will help you orient yourself after you've gone through it. For the longest time my life was BC and AC. Before China and After China. Moving to China was indeed such a significant transition that I orient myself in time according to it. My life as a public school teacher? BC. When did my parents first visit me in Chengdu? Two years AC. My sisters? Three years AC. When did I go to Vietnam the first time? Four years AC. When did longtime family friend Joe Brouwer as well as my grandma die? In my fifth year AC. This is how I think about time. Of course, if you were to ask me the year, I can figure it out. But the figuring will go through the BC/AC lens to this day.

It's natural for people to mark things in terms of before or after events: graduation, marriage, a certain job, a baby, a painful breakup, a big move, or a serious health issue. But those events don't become the story. They become a page in the story or possibly the beginning of a new chapter. They join a plot larger than the transition each one creates. Part of staying fertile, then, involves reminding yourself of the bigger picture—the bigger story—that came before and will live on after it.

The nature of your transitional experience is that your life is being uprooted. The story you tell yourself and others about this transition is crucial. Does your story incorporate the past with an eye to the future? Is it large enough to hold more than this chapter?

My most recent transition was from the field, and at times it felt like I was transitioning from myself. Who was I apart from

Looming Transitions

China? I thought my China story line was going to be longer, much longer. While loss was a strong part of the story, it was vital that I made room for other themes as well. As time has gone by, I can see them more clearly, but when I was at the point you are, I didn't know what they would be or how they would come to fruition. Instead, affirming that there was more to the story and that my story would move beyond just China helped.

When Moses returned from Mount Sinai with the Ten Commandments and gathered the people to instruct them, his teaching included the phrase, "So that you, your children, and their children after them may fear the Lord by keeping the commandments and so that you may enjoy long life."[16] Now, that's a pretty big story! It wasn't just about them, or the next generation; it was about future generations. Later, Moses reminded the people of the importance of remembering the bigger picture: when children ask, "What is the meaning of the law?" God's people should be able to answer with the story of how God freed them from Egypt and provided the law so that they could prosper.

Getting the story right was key to understanding the law. Getting the story right is key for us today as well. That's why you need to make sure you know the story of your transition. And more to the point, do you have it right? If not, what needs to be changed as you tell it? Part of finishing well is to stay grounded in something that will far outlive this transition. Staying rooted in Christ while being uprooted in this chapter of your story is going to be a daily reorienting point in the story you tell.

But times of transition are bumpy. Our spiritual lives are easier to ignore for the very reason mentioned above: God is the same yesterday, today, and tomorrow. You might notice that you begin to take God for granted. If he is going to be on the other side and screaming needs exist, at times incessantly, in the here-and-now, why not allow God to go before and prepare the way? And you'll catch up with him. How does one go about the lofty yet necessary goal of staying grounded in Christ? What does that even mean? Simply put, the connection you have with God must be maintained, even nurtured, and not simply put on

Stay Grounded in Christ

autopilot or shelved.

For some, staying connected to God will look similar both before and during the transition. For others, it will not. You may know at this point how it will go for you. This might be your first transition where you have to go it alone or you might not have had young children before or you might have been the one staying and now you're the one leaving. Responses to the demands of transitions vary, so have a plan and check in with yourself, a spouse, counselor, or friend and ask if what you are doing is still working. Are you still grounded in Christ? If not, what needs to be changed? When will be the next time you will check in with these confidants? Transitions can throw curveballs. Is it reasonable to check in once a week? Every two weeks? Once a month? Checking in might start out once a month and need to become more frequent as the transition approaches.

True maintenance of a relationship with God is spontaneous, unpredictable, vibrant, and active. You need to find a system that works with you and your personality. When you check in with someone, it could look like any one or a combination of the following:

- An actual checklist
- A ranking 1 to 10 scale with one being distant and ten being strongly grounded
- A journal
- A brief weekly email to one person or a small group
- Meeting for coffee or tea
- Talking on the phone or online via e-conference for thirty minutes to an hour
- If you are part of a small group, begin each session by discussing the status of your relationship with God.

Questions to cover include any of the following:

1. Do you seem to be grounded in Christ? How do you know?
2. What lessons have you been learning or have been rein-

forced—about God, yourself, your marriage, or a combination?
3. How do you see God at work in this transition?
4. What ways have you been disappointed recently with God?
5. In what ways might God have been disappointed with you lately?
6. What has made God smile when he thinks of you?

As you monitor this area, if you find you are grounded, wonderful. Truly. I pause now as I write this to picture you and smile. But often in times of transition, and especially as our routines begin to be anything but routine, times with God begin to slip away. If it does, don't beat yourself up over it. Experiment with ideas in this chapter and offer yourself permission to fail.

Big rocks on the spiritual pathway

You've probably heard of the analogy of "big rocks," but in case you haven't, picture a large glass jar, rocks, pebbles, sand and water. If you were asked to fill the jar with the rocks, pebbles, sand, and water, there are several ways you could go about putting them in. But if you wanted to fit all of them in, there is only one way all would fit: first rocks, then pebbles, then sand, and finally water. If you put the sand in and then the water, there wouldn't be room for the pebbles or rocks. It doesn't take a rocket scientist to figure out that the rocks stand for the important parts of life and need to go in the jar first. Your day-to-day life is represented by the pebbles and might not be the same week to week; and then the sand and water symbolize the ways you invest your time that has you scratching your head at the end of the day wondering where the day went. Who hasn't played a few more rounds of a game on the Internet or gone down the Facebook rabbit hole and lost chunks of time? If the big rocks are in place, an occasional tumble down the rabbit hole can be a welcome break.

Stay Grounded in Christ

In all of life, but especially when we are cultivating a fertile soul, staying grounded in Christ is a big rock and worth guarding. Part of guarding your relationship with God is knowing yourself and what may or may not work for you; it also involves getting creative and throwing some *shoulds* out the window: "I should read my Bible for twenty minutes a day"; "I *should* make time to help with the clothing drive at school"; "I *should* be reading a spiritual book a month"; "I *should* be able to cook homemade meals more often." My friend Patty shared this tip with a group of fellow cross-cultural workers. She asked us to write down a few of our *shoulds* and then to cross out the word *should* and write *could* instead. So, what *could* you do to stay connected to God?

In *God Is Closer Than You Think*, John Ortberg describes seven pathways in which people can connect with God: intellectual, relational, serving, worship, activist, contemplative, and creation. Because each one of us is different, no "right" way—or even a better way—exists to access God. That being said, you walk some of the pathways more often and more naturally than others. For me, I can gauge the effectiveness of a pathway for myself by noticing whether I come alive or start to count the minutes. For example, I'm not driven much by music unless I'm in an exercise class or alone in the car. In church, after three songs, I'm ready to move on. *Oh my word? Another song? For the love of all that is worshipful, can we please sit down?* Books, however, are my friends and provide a sense of being truly alive. About a week before I would return to the U.S. for a visit, I would log on to my local library and request eight to ten books I knew I wanted to read. Even jet lag couldn't squelch my joy in having books to read, knowing God would meet me in the pages with new ideas and inspiring writing.

Read through the following descriptions and see which two or three fit you most naturally:[17]

1. *Intellectual pathway*—If this is your pathway, you draw closer to God as you learn more about him. Practices like read-

ing and studying are important because the way to the heart is through the mind. However, in times of stress someone on this pathway can go too much into an analytic or problem-solving mode.

2. *Relational pathway* — If this is your pathway, being with people engages you. You have a deep sense of God's presence when you're involved in significant relationships. Ortberg cautions those on this path against two dangers. The first is superficiality due to being spread thin from too many relationships. The second is becoming a spiritual chameleon and relying too much on what others think.

3. *Serving pathway* — If this is your pathway, how you experience joy is through serving. God's presence seems most tangible when you're involved in helping others. The danger is to think that God is only present when you are serving, and the temptation is to resent those who don't serve as much.

4. *Worship pathway* — If this is your pathway, being involved in worship brings life and you have a natural gift for expression and celebration. Things to guard against are judging those who are not as expressive as you and looking for the next "worship high."

5. *Activist pathway* — If this is your pathway, you are passionately aware of God when mobilizing people in a cause. Your passion is to act. A caution if this is your primary pathway: in your zeal, be aware not to run over or exploit people in your pursuits.

6. *Contemplative pathway* — If this is your pathway, you have a large inner world and feel the presence of God most when alone. God is more present to you when distractions and noises are removed. Because of the reality of modern life and the added pressures that transition brings, you may need to follow this pathway more than in other seasons. At other times, realize that when disappointed and stressed you may be tempted to retreat. As John Ortberg said, "Involvement in significant relationships and regular acts of service will help keep you tethered to the external world."[18]

7. *Creation pathway* — If this is your pathway, you have a pas-

sionate ability to connect with God when you are experiencing the world he made. However, in times of stress and transition guard against using this pathway as an escape or a reason not to connect with others around you.

It is fairly clear I'm not on the worship pathway. As you read through the list, probably several jumped out as natural ways that you connect with God. How vast and broad our God is in the ways he communes with us! In addition, it's freeing to know we don't have to walk on all of the above paths. If music is not your thing, don't condemn yourself. Can you imagine if everyone primarily connected with God through song? Who would be out organizing the causes? Who would be writing books or cooking meals or going on prayer walks?

As I prepared to move back to the U.S., I knew I'd have to make hard choices about my books—a primary way I connect to God and myself. Before I started to dismantle and sort, I filmed a video in which I talked about how I had organized them and how much I loved them and would miss them. I can't believe how much that one act helped me honor their importance in my life and help me stay connected to God; he wasn't just asking me to give up the most treasured part of my apartment and life, he was mourning it with me. As I wrote this section, I re-watched the video and was back in the agony of the looming transition. But in watching the video and hearing the quiver in my voice as I got near the end of filming, I also felt connected to God once again. I am grateful he understood how much my bookshelves and books meant to me and that I needed to honor their role in my life to stay connected to him. (In the footnotes is a link to the video.[19])

In this season of transition, it will be vital for you to stay on one or more of the paths.[20] As mentioned earlier, your path might be the same one you were on before you knew you'd be leaving. Perhaps you have been in a Bible study group (intellectual and relational pathways) that meets twice a month and ends in a time of praying for one another (worship pathway).

Looming Transitions

The group may play a significant role in grounding you as the lessons you learn weave into the transition, helping you both to prepare for and process through it.

But sometimes in times of transition, you are not able to do what you had done before (or at least not in the same capacity). At these times, you need to be open to other pathways for this season. Maybe you are a contemplative person who is going to be moving away. While you might still need some time alone, this season may be one in which the Lord reaches out to you through others as you have more meals, parties, and coffee dates with people who want time with you before you leave. If this is the case, it will help you to redefine how you are being fed and to look for ways that God is meeting you and using you as you interact with others. Or if you are someone who naturally connects with God by serving others, you might need to allow others to serve you and then reflect (contemplative pathway) on what you are learning through being served.

When my friend Lisa decided to leave the field, I knew it was the right decision for her as she followed God's leading, but it would stink, stink, stink for me. Around that time I heard the song *My Life Would Suck Without You* on a TV show and even though it's about a dysfunctional romantic relationship, that line captured how I felt about the news. It's got a peppy beat and was perfect for the elliptical machine at the gym as I connected with God over how much I would miss Lisa.

Switching pathways can also take the form of being on the same pathway but interacting with it in a new way. Instead of reading a book over a morning cup of tea, you might listen to one as you drive around on a day of errands. Or instead of playing with the worship team at church, you might listen to worship music you haven't listened to in a long time. It's not so much about *what* you do or *which* pathway you are on. All are ways that can lead to connecting to God. In times of transition when much is out of your control, it is tempting either to keep doing what you've always done even if it doesn't seem to benefit you in the same way or to throw it out in frustration because it is no longer working. Right now, as you make decisions about how you want to approach this season of life, be open to going down other pathways.

Grounded in chocolate or Jesus?

The Bible contains analogies and reminders about the Kingdom of God being like a pearl *of great cost* and the importance of *counting the cost*. Just as a farmer invests much on the front end of the growing season with unknowns such as the weather or potential harvest help, staying grounded in Christ is like other mysterious paradoxes. You will tether yourself. You can tether yourself to your reputation, to a hobby, to avoidance, or to Jesus. Will your main tether hold during this stormy season? Another way to ask it is: Are you going to be grounded in Christ and supplementing with chocolate? Or grounded in chocolate and supplementing with Jesus?

Staying grounded in Jesus and supplementing with chocolate doesn't guarantee you will hear from God or feel close to him during the transition. God is not a cosmic vending machine. There might be times when you wonder if you ever heard from him at all or question if he cares or really has your best at heart. Does he get how painful this is? Parts of scripture address these deep and scary questions. The Psalms are rich with poems and conversations that bring voice to these questions. If God seems more distant than usual or than you would like at this time, reading through the Psalms can reassure you that you are not losing your mind. The Psalms may even provide specific verses or passages to claim and memorize. They can become prayers on your behalf.

If you are finding yourself not as grounded as you'd like and want to experiment with the different pathways, here are some ideas:

- Maintain routines such as going to church or participating in a small group.

Looming Transitions

- Read scriptures, devotionals, and/or books on spiritual development.
- Have a live plant or flowers around as visual reminders of Creation and the need to cultivate a fertile soul.
- Listen to podcasts, including sermons or on-line free theological classes.
- Listen to praise and worship music that helps you focus on God.
- Create a worship playlist specifically for this transition time.
- If you need to pack or downsize, use the sorting as a spiritual activity by reflecting on what you have been given, the people and experiences in your life that each item represents, and the next person who will be blessed by that item.
- Combine exercise with a spiritual practice such as listening to a sermon, connecting with a friend, or praying.
- Allow the tears to flow as you experience different emotions over the transition, such as sadness, excitement, frustration, hurt, and eagerness.
- Rest! Remember the rhythm that God placed within work and Sabbath. The Sabbath is for rest, reflection, and worship. Transitions are not known for being restful. Going into it, put rest on your to-do list as a part of what will keep you grounded in Christ. If you don't make it a priority, it will be one of the first things to be squeezed out.
- Set aside a certain time period each day during the transition to just be. It could be as short as five minutes or as long as thirty minutes. During that time just sit and be. If your thoughts are running wild, command them to stop for this time, visualize yourself turning down a volume button in your brain, or try to slow them down with deep breathing.

When a farmer talks about how fertile a field is, it is with an eye beyond *this* season or *this* particular crop. Not so with

Stay Grounded in Christ

the sporadic backyard gardener who means well. Certainly she does things to help, such as creating a fertile environment for the tomatoes or beans she has planted, looking forward to enjoying the fruits of her labor. But most likely her primary goal is the harvest at the end of the season. Both the farmer and the gardener grow something. Both invest time, effort, worry, and love into their plants. But the difference lies in the story they tell, not the plants themselves. For the gardener, the story is about *these* plants and *this* season, but for the farmer it is about this *field* and the various crops it has produced in the past and will produce in the future.

You will outlive this season. May God infuse you with the faith and hope to speak of it in ways that point to these truths as you stay connected to him. Now that we have a key big rock in place, staying grounded in Christ, it's time to add another one, and this one will add light and levity and just may turn you into a comedian.

Chapter Four

Laughter Revives the Soul

If you tickle the earth with a hoe she laughs with a harvest.
—Douglas William Jerrold

A joyful heart is good medicine, But a broken spirit dries up the bones.
—Proverbs 17:22

If my life were made into a movie (and don't we all secretly hope to live a life so interesting others will want to watch it?), I can picture how the shuttle scene from the introduction might play out for the audience: it's a sweet scene, so someone watching it would innocently reach for a piece of popcorn as I, just as innocent, board the shuttle, eager to return to my beloved Kansas. In my mind the viewer would nearly choke on said popcorn when the "kind" stranger moves to sit next to Sandra Bullock (who is a natural to play me because we both have brown hair) and comments to me on my distraught state. Cringe.

It is so uncomfortable.

It is.

Why return to it and make us all cringe again?

Because as the movie continues, it would show this story beginning to take on a new life. After arriving in Kansas I retold it. Um, a lot. The first time I retold it, I was speaking to a decent-sized audience who had gathered on a Sunday evening to hear about my work and upcoming transition back to the field. It is the kind of story that gets good mileage. You can picture

Laughter Revives the Soul

the reactions in the audience as I got to the punch line. A comedic pregnant pause led those listening to wonder what the stranger would say. And when she said "distraught," there was a collective gasp as the audience members put themselves in the story and related to the uncomfortable feeling of being called distraught. By a stranger. In front of other strangers. Can we say awkward with a capital A? But after the collective gasp, what was the reaction? Probably the same as yours.

Admit it, you probably chuckled or at least smiled a little bit as you pictured it, even if only in your heart (because you, too, are "kind" and might not want to laugh outright). Let's face it, while that incident is awkward, it's also kind of funny. Now, it may not be the funniest thing you've ever heard and the actual experience of it wasn't overtly humorous. But it has the making of a good story because you can imagine the experience either as the woman weeping or one of the businessmen not sure what to do.

Why not laugh now?

You are probably reading this in some sort of temperature-controlled environment, whether by heat in the winter or air conditioning in the hot summer, depending where you are. Guess where farming usually does not happen? Inside, in temperature-controlled environments. It is not breaking news that farming is exhausting work, involving long hours and work conditions that are whatever the Good Lord provides, regardless of what the weather channel predicts. No matter how inspirational the bigger story is, sometimes it is not particularly inspirational in the here and now of *this* particular day.

The big picture can be just that: big. Sometimes too big. On those long hard days in the sun, being revived comes in the simple form of a short rest and a cool drink. So it is with the soul.

As I said earlier, you must have the trustworthy big picture: the transition you are in is not the sum of your story. This belief is foundational, but on certain days when the sun is blaring

Looming Transitions

down in the form of tasks to be completed, decisions to be made, and people to see, the bigger story is too "out there" and philosophical. In those moments, what the body and soul needs is a dose of revival through a chuckle.

My friend Joann has a great line: if you are going to laugh later, why not laugh now? And this is another piece of keeping your soul fertile: find ways to laugh at yourself or at the situations you will find yourself in. Often the "right" answer about what revives you as a Christian involves "holy" activities. I'm using quotation marks because I'm pushing back on the narrow ideas of what is "right" or "holy." One of God's greatest gifts to us is laughter. Appropriate laughter is able to wed the awkward/annoying/hurtful with the surreal/humorous/can-you-believe-that-really-happened. In most situations, multiple layers occur at once and appropriate humor (not at the expense of another) sparks the integration of these layers by acknowledging they both exist. If the grief and the awkwardness can be wed, it brings levity without swinging to one extreme or the other.

And so we return to the ball perched atop the point, wanting to roll to one side or the other. The stress of these situations can be relieved by being lost either in the grieving aspect at the expense of any humor or on cheap laughs at the expense of pain. But if the two can be embraced at the same time and brought into a shared space, neither are elevated or ignored. The two are integrated yet still separate. The grief doesn't cease to exist nor is it less uncomfortable, but there is levity. This can be the beauty of laughter: it creates space for more than just a laugh.

A fertile soul facing a transition is one that is able to hold both the pain of the losses *and* the humorous as well as embrace difficult moments that will come. Sure, there will be times when you fall more to one side or the other. If you're going to laugh later, why not look for a way to laugh now? This will come more easily to some than to others, but it is something that can be cultivated in anyone. It is not simply that some people see the lighter side of situations and others don't. If you don't tend to laugh easily, you can train yourself to notice the humorous aspects in

Laughter Revives the Soul

most situations.

Let me take a moment to explain that I am not looking for a cheap laugh. This isn't laughter for laughter's sake. Sometimes laughter is an attempt to process shocking news, like Sarah's reaction in Genesis to the news that she would be pregnant. Sarah's laughter was born out of something positive: a long-desired and imagined pregnancy that would soon become reality. Other times laughter can help soften the blow of something decidedly less positive.

My friend Amy had a high school foreign exchange student from Southeast Asia live with her and her family for a year. He took over the guest bedroom for a year and in preparation she put most of the room's decorations in storage, but left out a few, including a framed one-of-a-kind profile cutout of her son from when he was a young boy. To make Van feel the space was his too, she bought him his own picture frame to use. After he returned to his home country, Amy discovered that instead of using the new picture frame she had gotten him as well, he had thrown out her son's one-of-a-kind profile cutout and put a picture in it (when he left he took his picture). He did, however, leave the frame with "Sample Photo" untouched. The cutout is gone, and it is a loss that cannot be retrieved. Amy can't make another one, as her son is much older now and the cutout would not be the same. She was able to mourn the loss while also seeing the humor of now having a frame stock photo as a "family heirloom."

Fertile soul laughter in times of transition isn't laughing in order to mask or deny a loss, and often it cannot be the first response. But it is able to tap into more than just the pain.

Laughter that acknowledges a range of emotions encapsulated in one place will be fostered as you look for both sides: the reasonable and the absurd, the pain and the humor, the deep and the superficial, the material loss and the gain in perspective. If this isn't your default, begin to train yourself to tune into details that will flesh out what is going on.

Below are two versions of the same incident I experienced at the doctor's office. As you read, consider this question: which version helps to capture the two aspects that we have been talking about and hold them in tension, ultimately allowing for levity?

A: Today at the doctor's I nearly died of embarrassment.

OR

B: Today at the doctor's office I explained to the nurse that I need to be tested for syphilis, hepatitis, AIDS, and tuberculosis to get a work visa in China. During my examination with the doctor, we talked about how expensive it can be to move overseas. As we were leaving the examination room, the doctor glanced at my chart and unexpectedly said to virtually everyone who happened to be gathered around the nurses' station: "Based on your medical history there is no need to be tested for TB, hepatitis, syphilis, or AIDS. They are expensive, so let's cancel them and save you some money!" I squeaked out, "No, no, I do need to be tested," as I made a beeline for the door.

Both are true and accurate versions of the same event, but version B invites people in to the tension and the levity. The difference between the two is found in the details. And it is in the details that the soul is revived. As you recall and share stories of experiences you're having as you prepare for your transition, keep in mind that paying attention to and including details does not necessarily correlate with length. However, in the above examples, the more humorous version B is certainly longer than version A.

Someone can go on and on without saying much or use very few words but say a lot. It's the ability to include enough without overdoing it. In the example above, what time of day was it? What was the doctor wearing? How many people were at the nurses' station? Those details aren't included because they would get in the way and cause the listener to become confused

Laughter Revives the Soul

about which details to pay attention to. Instead, the awkwardness—in fact, the humor—is in the tension between the doctor trying to save money, me needing to get the appropriate tests, and the different understanding of what the appropriate tests were. Thus, those details are included, allowing the listener to focus on them and thereby "get" the point of the story.

Who are some of the good storytellers in your life? I bet they are people who know how to give enough details for people to engage with the story without losing, confusing, or boring people. Sometimes more is just more, and sometimes less is just less. The paradox of "less is more" really is about the right kind of less leading to more. But it is in the details that we are able to share our experiences—and therefore our loads—with others.

We have said that this type of laughter isn't just about a cheap laugh, and it isn't. The point is that our souls are revived by laughter or the joy in knowing that we are not alone. Revived. When you read that word, what happens to you? Read it again.

Revived.

Not to ruin the calm feeling you have now, but let's talk about grammar. The word *grammar* probably doesn't have quite the calming effect as *revived*. Ignoring that for the moment, it is our unpopular friend *grammar* who will provide an insight that might otherwise be missed as we look at *revive*.

Revive can be both a transitive and an intransitive verb. Please stick with me; this is important *and* interesting! Really. The difference lies in whether or not the verb needs an object to receive the action. "'Trans' means to carry. 'In' as a prefix means 'not.' A transitive verb has to 'carry' the action from the subject to the complement."[21] Fearing you might doubt me on how interesting this is, two examples will help. First, the word *broke*. I can't just yell at someone, "I broke!" without looking either ridiculous or like I am mocking my financial state. Something was broken, and I broke it: a dish, a bone, a promise, or someone's heart. Something needs to be there to be broken; thus, *broke* is a transitive verb. However, some verbs can stand alone and don't require an object. If I were to yell "Bolt!" after you misgauged on-

Looming Transitions

coming traffic (true story, my sister Laura yelled this at me, our other sister, and to top it off, our blind friend), you don't need an object to complete the action as you start running for your life. Your movement would show the fact that *bolt* is an intransitive verb: there is nothing to receive the action.

Some verbs are strictly either transitive or intransitive, while others can be both. *Revive* is one of the lucky verbs that can be both. Returning to the good feeling we had before all this talk of grammar, Merriam-Webster provides the following definition and distinction of revive:[22]

Intransitive verb: to return to consciousness or life; become active or flourishing again

Transitive verb:
1. to restore to consciousness or life
2. to restore from a depressed, inactive, or unused state: bring back
3. to renew in the mind or memory

Both the intransitive and transitive parts contain the same basic idea of returning, renewing, or restoring. There will be times that laughter revives you in an intransitive sense when you simply are revived, returned from that crazed person you were. Revived, you become again someone who can deal with strangers, spouses, children, and friends as bumps in your transitions come along. When you are revived, it is like listening to a well-played piece of music where all the notes are struck in the proper order.

Being in a revived state seems to enhance the essence of everything. A diet coke is even more refreshing than normal. The sky is blue, really blue. Your wife is indeed the woman you thought you married. Your children are not minions of Satan, just over-exhausted and in need of a little TLC. It's like when you were a kid lying in the backyard with the smell of freshly cut grass in the air, the warm sun on your skin, and not a care

Laughter Revives the Soul

in the world, except now you are an adult, and while you might have more than a few "cares in the world," they don't seem as daunting thanks to being revived. You are back. You are you. And you can make it on your own.[23]

Other times laughter revives *transitively* in that something specific is revived. As something is revived, it can either be restored or renewed. You're probably about done with grammar, but a few examples will help, and I promise you'll feel revived.[24] Revival can be experienced in the following areas:

- **Hope**—Revival can bring hope that you won't always be faced with these decisions, that you aren't alone in this, or that no matter what comes at you, it won't be more than you can bear with God and the help of others.
- **Attitude**—Revival can remind you that maybe, just maybe, the whole world isn't stacked against you, that this *is* doable and may even have good come of it, that people can be counted on and trusted.
- **Relationships**—Revival can teach you that while the relationships you are in may be strong and healthy, a good laugh (especially at yourself) can lighten the mood and bring people closer; tensions can lessen and space for treating each other kindly is created or enlarged.
- **Strength**—Revival can bring strength to face what it is that you need to confront, to finish the tasks that you need to do, to make the decisions that you need to make, and to keep moving until all is done.
- **Health**—Revival through laughter can improve health. In short, your muscles are more relaxed, your digestive system works better, and you are able to exercise and sleep in healthy amounts.
- **Sense of control**—Revival can bring the situation under control by being able to laugh at ourselves or the situation.
- **Perspective**—Revival results in greater perspective: that others have it rough too, that you aren't alone, that what you are facing will be temporary, and maybe (perhaps,

Looming Transitions

perchance, conceivably, 'tis possible) you have been a bit more of a drama queen or king than normal.

The gift that keeps on giving

So far we have talked about the importance of recognizing and tapping into two realms at once: the awkward/annoying/hurtful part of an experience and the surreal/humorous/can-you-believe-that-really-happened part. The ability to integrate them is the beginning of revival. We have also looked at the importance of details, the distinction of showing versus telling, helping the person you are sharing with to enter in and relate. The final piece is having someone to share your stories with.

My experience on the shuttle bus didn't begin to revive me until I began to share it with others. Until it was given form in the retelling, it was mostly embarrassing and awkward, and I would have preferred to pretend it didn't happen. The retelling allowed me to see the shuttle ride from the outside. I watched the faces of those listening to me, and I was able to join with them in responding with distress and a good laugh. It was in the sharing that it moved from *awkwardness and shame* to *awkwardness and funny*. The burden was lifted just a bit as levity infused the experience.

Recently I recounted an uncomfortable story with a friend over the phone. A few days later she shared that as she picked up dog poop outside and recalled our conversation, she found herself chuckling over our conversation. She found herself chuckling over it again—though she assured me she doesn't only think of me while picking up dog poop. The image of her outside in the cold of winter chuckling over something that happened in another corner of the world, not related to her own life, enabled both of us to be refreshed (and, as a bonus, a nasty task was made more tolerable).

Finding someone to share your story can take on many forms. It can happen during a phone call to a friend or over lunch with a colleague. But there is also something powerful and almost

Laughter Revives the Soul

magical about sharing with a group. Consider the groups you are a part of through work, school, your team, an online community, or church and be willing to share with them.

Several years ago my mom had, shall we say, an "incident" with the deli man at the local supermarket. He asked her how she was and instead of answering the question, she placed her order. The deli man said, "I asked you how you are, when you tell me I'll serve you." Feeling a bit annoyed at being bullied she did an about-face and went to talk to his manager. Mom shared this incident with her book group, a group in which many of the members shopped at the store and knew the deli man themselves. Although he was kind of a pill to Mom, he wasn't the only one in the encounter who could be a pill, and the book club knew this. Because she was willing to share with the other women—and then later with other family and friends—her communities could join in and experience the incident themselves. It's even been dubbed "Marsha and the deli man." Whenever anyone says that phrase now, a chuckle is had and a small bit of revival washes over the room. She took an annoying and potentially shameful interaction and used it as a point of connection.

If you're living overseas, you might be in a situation where you read the above and think of the groups you *don't* have. Instead, focus on what you do have. Do you regularly eat lunch with teammates? Are you part of a homeschooling co-op? Do you know any other folks preparing to go to the field or leave it? You can share through text messages, blogs, or social media. The key is to find someone to share with—it doesn't need to be public, and certain situations require discretion. However, the key is this: keeping your soul fertile requires you don't go it alone.

Lead the way

There is one more ingredient. Okay, so something has happened in your season of transition. You've had an encounter or an unexpected bump on the path, and you're going to let someone in on it. As you share it, be quick to join in on the laugh. In finding the humor in a situation, there will be a bit of awkwardness as people won't always be sure how to respond. Do you mean for them to laugh? Will you be insulted or hurt if they laugh? We've all been in those situations when we weren't sure what to do. But as you lead with your own laughter first, you give them permission to join in. It's great to be around people who are secure enough in themselves to let others laugh both at and with them. The paradox is that as you extend this gift to others, you will receive more than you give.

That being said, not all situations have a lighter side. Some are just plain awful. There is nothing funny about being told your child has cancer, you lost your job, or your friend miscarried . . . again. This isn't a principle to apply to all of life. But in a transition where you need to let places and roles die to create space for new to grow, there *will* be some lighter moments. In the midst of stress, pockets of shade away from the blazing sun exist. Look for them. Recognize them. Share them. Enjoy them.

You're going to need them as we get ready to look at the next part of your transition.

Chapter 5

Accept That It's Going to Be Messy

If you pray for rain, be prepared to deal with some mud.
—Mary Englebreit

Accept doesn't mean like.
—Amy Young

It's funny what you miss from your home culture when you move overseas. For me, it is freshly cut grass. In particular, the smell of freshly cut grass.

What is it about a freshly cut lawn that is so refreshing that I begin to relax at the thought of the smell? I might have over-romanticized this because the few times I'd smell freshly cut grass in China, body and soul jumped into action. I had to stop and sniff where the smell might be coming from since I couldn't see it. It was rare to smell it in China, making cut grass almost sacred.

The person behind the mower can relish in the satisfaction of a job well done. It's a job where it is easy to see and measure and celebrate progress, unlike so many jobs in modern life where it is not so evident when a job is complete—unlike the work you have been or will be doing. Yet it is also a job that brings the joy of announcing itself through the air and shares its news freely with any who would breathe. "I have been recently cut. Come join in my freshness!"

Looming Transitions

As is evident from these ramblings, I love a well-mowed lawn. Mowing is, without a doubt, my favorite outdoor warm-weather job. Whether I have mowed or someone else has, I just like the sense of a job done, the shade of green on the freshly mowed grass tips, the smell, the freshness, the sense of hope. I recall stopping with a few fellow Americans near a rarely spotted mowed lawn in Beijing—a hush fell over us as we inhaled and released a pleasurable sigh. Maybe a mowed lawn does not call out to you in such a manner or with such love, and you might wonder what special hold mowing has on me. When a newly moved lawn calls out and invites me to join in her freshness, she also whispers to the dark recesses of my heart and reminds me why she'll always hold a special place with me: "What other yard tasks keep dirt from getting under your nails?"

There you have it. While I love being outside and am willing to work hard, I abhor the feeling of dirt under my fingernails. Even just thinking about it right now is actually giving me shivers. Setting that aside, we come to another part of keeping your soul fertile as you finish well: accept that it's going to be messy. You are going to get some metaphorical dirt under your nails. Of course, there are things you can do to help minimize the dirt, but even if you find the most perfect pair of gardening gloves, there are just some tasks that you can't do wearing gloves. Part of the finishing well is accepting that it is simply going to be messy both physically and emotionally.

What are your goals – both stated and unstated?

Recently some friends were moving from Beijing to another city and had scheduled the movers to arrive on the last Wednesday afternoon they would be in town. Imagine all of our surprise when a large truck and six workers showed up on Tuesday afternoon, a good twenty-four hours before expected. While the initial reaction was to say, "Um, we have an agreed upon time and you'll just have to come back tomorrow," the reality was the movers were driving that night to the destination city (and this

Accept That It's Going to Be Messy

was in China, so pointing to the contract wasn't going to get us far[25]). Did they want their stuff on the moving truck or not? It wasn't the time to start debating the fine print or the principle of the matter. It was time to finalize packing and get furniture and boxes loaded up! I don't care how well you prepare, how many lists you make, how much you think through all of the things that need to be done between now and then, there will still be muddled situations.

Another aspect to finishing well is accepting that you can't or won't do it (whatever "it" is) perfectly. Allowing something to come to an end so that there is space for something new is simply going to involve grime. What farmer returns from a long day in the field looking exactly like he did when he went out the door in the morning? The obvious answer is the one who didn't do any farming. It's a lot of work to prepare a field for a new crop, and while some facets will be cleaner than others—a farmer with a cup of coffee in hand paging through a seed catalog versus a farmer churning up the soil—at some point every farmer will have to go outside and do some of the messier parts of farming. In preparing a field for a new crop to be planted, the old needs to be cleared away, and the earth turned up. Some of the turning is relatively easy and effortless, but when you work with dirt, the chances are pretty high you'll get dirty. Likewise, going through a transition is going to be messy.

Most people harbor unrealistic expectations about transitions, assuming that they can or will "do it" perfectly. Let's consider the assumptions you may have about a perfect transition (and therefore the standards you might be holding yourself and others to):

- No one is unhappy (including children, grandparents, and yourself).
- Everything happens on time.
- There are no financial surprises, and everything is under budget.
- Everyone is impressed with the way you handle every-

thing.
- All goes according to plan.
- Everyone agrees with every decision you make.
- There is a pervasive sense of calm and serenity at all times in your home.
- Emotions and reactions are always appropriate.

Turn on the lights because our fantasy movie has come to an end, and it's time to re-enter the real world. As you read through the above list, do you notice a theme? All of the statements contain extreme words: no one, every, all, and always. Is it reasonable to expect *all* to go according to your plan? Well, when it's stated so clearly, no, it's not. Or how about *everyone* agreeing with *every* decision you make? How often do all members of the same family want to go out for the same kind of food? If you have kids, you'll know it happens about as often as your fairy godmother showing up with dinner. Most of us would say out loud that we don't expect everything to go perfectly, but then act blindsided when they don't. The truth is most of us have realistic expectations for others—because that's just real life—but when it comes to ourselves, we somehow think the laws of nature or the odds of something bad happening enter a vortex and do not apply to us. Although we might never say it out loud because we don't even realize we're thinking that way, we secretly think those bad things won't happen to us.

Or maybe you are the opposite and you're thinking, are you crazy?! Of course, this transition is going to be a disaster! Because in your world you live under a cloud, like Charlie Brown in the *Peanuts* cartoon, and feel you can't escape bad things happening. Why? Because things never work out for you. You are the one who believes if there is going to be a problem, it will happen to you. You are always the one who gets charged more, loses something, or gets taken advantage of. It's normal to have secret, even subconscious expectations. The biggest surprise may come because you don't recognize your own expectations

Accept That It's Going to Be Messy

until they come out through your reactions. It's like you have been keeping a secret from yourself. It's not a bad secret, just something that was so obvious to "you" it never occurred to "you" to share it with yourself until now.

Recognize a pattern here? This way of thinking is just as extreme as Ms. or Mr. Pollyanna above, but in the opposite direction with the default being everything will go *perfectly* wrong. Either way, all good or all bad, under the stress of transition, thinking patterns are exposed.

Remember the ball balanced on top of the point? It is one of the laws of nature to want to relieve tension by going to one extreme or the other because the other option (living with the tension) is wearisome. And yet that is what mature adults do: learn to live with the tension.[26]

Going into the transition, the main goal is not to uncover every secret belief you have. Hopefully you know yourself well and have already worked on adjusting your expectations. If you haven't, it would be helpful to think through some of the expectations you listed in Chapter Two? However, working through the exercises and becoming as aware of expectations as you can, you won't be able to unearth all of them. That is why tuning in to your reactions is a key component of finishing well. It is in your reactions that the gap between your expectations and reality is exposed and therefore able to be identified and addressed. We've already looked at expectations, but it's worth briefly revisiting the subject.

People are going to disappoint, things are going to cost more time and money than you would like, you might underestimate how many boxes you need for packing, and you may become a crazed person when these things occur. In other words, it's going to be messy. Accept this. You are still responsible for planning well and holding up your end of things, but a sign of finishing well is the ability to embrace the chaos of life. As Mary Englebreit says, "If you pray for rain, be prepared to deal with some mud." In terms of finishing well, if something is coming to an end, be prepared to deal with the mess.

Where messes may hide

The messiness of finishing well can come in expected and unexpected places: relationships, housing and possessions, finances, and weather.

Relationships

One-size-fits-all doesn't exist when it comes to relational messiness; instead the type of muck will be influenced by the relationship. For instance, those who are married will often have different assignments on the field. One of them may be responsible for the home while the other has a more "traditional" job working for the agency. For the sake of linguistic clarity, let's say that the husband is the one with the more clearly defined job and the wife will be in charge of their home life. However, they are leaving a healthy and known community, and she will need to start all over without the benefit of a new job to help jumpstart the process. This can create stress between them.

Tricky situations can also be seen in friends and family members who have unrealistic expectations about the amount of time you will be able to give them when the actual end comes into sight. Throw in some kids who are processing this differently than each other and suddenly the mess can be a little overwhelming. Messiness doesn't mean that one person is clearly right or wrong or that sin has occurred; it also doesn't mean it hasn't. It often shows up in hurt feelings, unmet expectations, and disagreements. Just yesterday I was talking with a cross-cultural work pastor, and he said the greatest problem of most cross-cultural workers is that they don't know how to relate and connect with other people. Instead, they know how to put on masks and pretend, which over time leads to isolation. So, when I say it's going to be relationally messy, that's not a statement of critique; messiness is part of being human.

Knowing relational chaos is likely to occur, be on the alert. Instead of having a "free pass" mentality where you expect special grace from people around you, you need to have a heightened

Accept That It's Going to Be Messy

awareness. If you notice yourself being mean, rude, snappish, cutting, cold, passive or passive-aggressive, you need to own up to it and make it right with those around you. If you notice others behaving this way toward you, it is appropriate for you to extend them grace, for the very nature of grace means it's not to be expected. Be quick to extend grace, but if you see behavior continuing, also be prepared to confront in love. They may or may not be aware that they are behaving badly.

One area that can be especially challenging regarding relationships involves decisions over whom you give your time to as your transition draws near. If you are moving, people will inevitably start to come out of the woodwork before you leave. A guiding principle is to invest more in relationships that have meant a great deal to you. This is something you will need to remind yourself before your transition. It's likely that in the final two weeks, people may start popping up, wanting to spend time with you. If you have been operating by the principle that important relationships take priority, it will help you to know whom to say yes to and whom to say no to. I also recognize cultural rules are in play, and you'll need to factor those in as well.

Housing and Possessions

I've put these two together because they usually go hand in hand: we keep our possessions, for the most part, in our homes. Housing can be one of the most stressful parts of finishing well, because our homes are where we store our earthly treasures and many memories. I've mentioned it before, but I'm not kidding when I say my bookshelves in my Beijing apartment rooted me there. This area is strongly influenced by whether you are going to the field and have a house you own, are on the field and transitioning to a new location, or are leaving the field permanently (at least for now). The more you can get settled now, the better. I have seen multiple individuals and couples on the field distracted and in a few cases, sadly, needing to leave the field because a house back home never sold or there was a problem with the renters. (I've also seen great blessings in this area!)

Looming Transitions

I don't know what the tumultuous part will look like for you—whether the sale of your home will fall through at the last minute, or whether the store will run out of the color of paint you need to finish repainting the bedrooms, or whether the housing market will be terrible in your area. But I can say with relative confidence, surprises will exist and they will be felt more acutely because they involve the home. The place that is supposed to be a sanctuary from problems now becomes the source of them.

And we haven't even begun discussing the earthly treasures we store within our homes. For some this will be an opportunity to downsize or to get rid of items you've been meaning to go through for some time. For others the thought of going through all of your things and deciding what to throw away, give away, sell, store, and pack is almost paralyzing. The answers to these questions will vary depending on whether this is a permanent move or a move for a season and whether you are leaving from or returning to your home country. A transition is a time when we recognize the hold that our stuff can have on us. It's also a time when stress means the brain might not be fully engaged, leading to certain heirlooms being passed on inadvertently.

Dealing with our things can be the rapids in the river of life. If you can stay in the raft, you can ride it out and you'll live to see calmer waters. Too many people experience wounds from getting bucked out and banged on the rocks. It will help to remind yourself (and others) that they are just things. If you find yourself having a strong reaction regarding your possessions, look behind the reaction for what might be going on at a deeper level. Is there sadness at a loss? Jealousy? Some form of betrayal or injustice? Is the message behind the reaction that these items say something about your value? Or a relationship? Sometimes what's really going on inside of you is relatively easy to identify, and sometimes it isn't. If you're not sure what's going on, take the time to reflect on your reactions and pay attention to what the Holy Spirit is telling you. He may speak to you through what you're reading, hearing, or talking about with others.

I wrote the following in a newsletter after I returned to China

Accept That It's Going to Be Messy

following a three-year study leave:

> Three years ago when I was packing up my apartment, I separated my things into boxes of "if I die, mail this to my family" and "if I die, open, go through, and get rid of." It's been interesting to see what three years ago I thought I would want now. I can objectively admit my family is fortunate I didn't die because they would have been mailed a bunch of stuff that would not have meant a hoot to them! I pity the person who would have opened the box of about 40 cassette tapes. Actually, they would have been able to throw them away without batting an eye. I, however, was only able to weed about eight out for the trash because so many have strong memories attached. They brought back parts of my life journey and I wept at the thought of throwing them away. Without them, what will remind me of those times and places? As you can see, I have been a bit too existential and dramatic in my thinking . . . a little too concerned about, well, frankly, *me*. I know we all want to live, and even leave behind us lives of significance. In packing up, leaving, and getting settled again, I am struck by the places I have overtly and secretly hidden where I get my significance and security. Sadly it isn't as consistently in the One who will never change as I would like. But, He too is gracious, and so it is guilt free that I have about 32 cassette tapes if you want to borrow some rocking 80's music.

You're not alone as you face your possessions. It was only in the last move that I was able to part with the cassette tapes. Since many had been mailed to me in my early years in China, they helped to carry my story, but their time had come to an end.

Finances

Finances are not just about money. Oh, that it were so simple. Finances are the door opening to a room that holds your values; in this room, you'll find your sense of security, and the idea of where worth comes from, and your belief about how time and effort should be invested. These are weighty and significant. So, when we talk about finances, we are actually talking about security, worth, and investment of resources. Is it any wonder that finances have the potential for messiness? There are three key points to remember when it comes to finances:

1. Transitions cost. Plain and simple, it is almost impossible for a phase of life to come to an end and another to start up without it costing you something. Be honest and realistic with yourself as to what you will need to pay for and how much things will cost. And then plan for it to cost more and add a 10 percent cushion to your budget.
2. Most people tend to fall in one of two categories: spenders or savers. Know which one you are and which one you are in a relationship with (child or spouse). Do not let money become more important than that relationship. Pure and simple: people trump money. Spending doesn't trump saving and saving doesn't trump spending. Relationships trump both.
3. One of the best pieces of advice I got from my parents concerning money is some problems are best solved by throwing a little money at them. Notice the key word "some." Not all problems need money thrown at them. In times of transition, there will be some situations where a little bit more money will save a lot of effort and maybe prevent headaches. Be willing to consider this as one way to solve a problem, but also build in some checks and balances to avoid throwing money at all problems.

Weather

The potential frustration with weather can be summed up in these two quotations:

> *"Climate is what we expect, weather is what we get."*
> — *Mark Twain*[27]

Accept That It's Going to Be Messy

"The trouble with weather forecasting is that it's right too often for us to ignore it and wrong too often for us to rely on it."
— Patrick Young[28]

As one of the masters of saying much with few words, Mark Twain aptly notes where messiness is located: in the gap between what is expected and what is delivered. Patrick Young (no relation) also gets it right by pointing out the weather is knowable. It's not all guesswork, and science is involved, but it's not like buying a Diet Coke from a vending machine in which you see your selection fall out after pushing a button. Weather chaos is not limited to one season or region; maddeningly, it can show up anywhere, anytime, and in many disruptive forms. It can rain on the day that you have a garage sale or plan to move. How does a freak blizzard sound on the weekend of your goodbye party? Or the largest hail storm to hit the county in a decade, leading to no electricity when you plan to back up all of your computer files? You need not become a pessimist, but remind yourself that weather is what we get and not the climate that we can expect.

A friend who read this in the months leading up to her move responded to this section with the following:

> "I had a little chuckle to myself last week, which was much needed as I was way too stressed out, when it rained all morning here in the city of no rain. And I remembered what you wrote on weather. That rainfall that morning which would normally not be any big deal at all—in fact welcomed—was all of a sudden too much for me to handle, and I realized I was feeling in over my head and like things were out of control. What it always boils down to for me, and what I appreciate about where you always focus and ground things, is whether or not I am staying close to the Lord through every moment. And I can see how, as soon as I let a much needed moment for pause with God slip away in order to accommodate getting something done, how flustered I become."

Looming Transitions

Weather can make it messy. Think through a few contingency plans, remind yourself that weather can make memories, and find the humorous side in what's happening.

Where do you cry in secret?

The four areas—relationships, housing and possessions, finances, and weather—are relatively external. But messiness can lurk within you, too. In the months leading up to the end of my time in Denver and the upcoming move back to China, I found myself crying almost every time I drove alone. I'd get in the car and even if I hadn't been thinking about the move or really about anything at all, I'd realize there were tears running down my cheeks. I'd be indeed thinking of some aspect of the move and often of something I'd really miss. As I'd near my destination, I'd tell myself to pull it together and do my best not to arrive with the obvious signs of crying. I felt like a hose that had sprung a leak. No matter what I tried, I just couldn't stop crying in my car. Almost regardless of my mood, the music I played, or other thoughts that were floating around, I leaked. I didn't like leaking. I felt out of control, and it was not timely at all. I had things that needed to be done, and there were still *several months* before I was to leave. Was I going to become a veritable fountain if this continued? What was up with the timing?

This thinking began an inner dialogue about the components of a well-timed emotional reaction. Some might think crying alone in the car was perfectly timed because others don't see you crying. Does well-timed mean you won't be embarrassed by the amount of time your emotional reaction lasts? Who wants to be the person who cries, blows up, clams up, or storms out of the room, regardless of how short or long the response is? No one wants to be that person. Or live with that person. And herein lies another aspect to the messiness of finishing well: the uncomfortable reality that our emotions are often more out of control than normal. Well-timed reactions are tidy and won't leave you feeling like an unexpected guest showed up, knocked on your door,

Accept That It's Going to Be Messy

and entered before you had time to realize what had happened.

Of course you want to have emotions because the alternative is either being like a pithed frog in science class, brain dead but kept alive for observation, or a robot. Brené Brown says we can't turn down the painful emotions without turning down the positive ones.[29] But that doesn't mean that you want to have them right *here* or right *now* or in front of *these* people!

The, shall we say, untidiness of emotions may show up in a variety of forms. For some it will involve crying more than normal, while others will have shorter fuses. And joy upon joy, the same person may have a host of reactions in the same day. Unreasonable one day (or moment) and weeping the next. It might be easier if you just picked one and stuck with it—at least people would know what to expect. But emotions don't work that way. Again, accept the mess.

Don't confuse accepting with liking. You can accept without liking it. Emotions are part of the way we have been made in the image of God. To have them is a good thing. To have them as fallen beings in a fallen world can be a messy thing.

The point in acceptance: freedom

The beauty of accepting is not that you have to declare the glass to be either half full or half empty; it is not that you become an existential realist on the alert for the next weather emergency that will bring rain to your parade. No. The beauty is that you are now freed to enjoy the mess.

One of the gifts passed on to me by my mother was dancing in the rain. In the late afternoon rain showers of my youth, when other mothers called their children to come in out of the rain, mine passed out umbrellas to my sisters and me and led us out to splash in the gutters. Shrieking with joy as the rain filled the gutters and ran over our bare feet, we ran into the reality of the weather instead of seeking to escape it.

Accepting messiness is not about becoming Eeyore. It is about embracing life so that in the midst of the mess, there can be joy as well.

Chapter 6

Know Yourself

It is not only the most difficult thing to know oneself, but the most inconvenient one, too.
—H.W. Shaw

Search me, God, and know my heart; test me and know my anxious thoughts.
—Psalm 139:23

When I moved from Chengdu to Beijing, the hardest part was going from a community where I was known to one where I was sort-of-known. Oh, plenty of people knew who I was, but they didn't really *know* me. Here we bump into the very frustrating limitations of the word "to know" in English. *Knowing* the capital of Colorado is quite different from *knowing* others deeply and being deeply *known*. I went from a deep and satisfying pool to new waters where I found myself drowning in a sea of shallowness. During this season of my life, Psalm 139 became a life preserver.

Psalm 139 starts and ends with the idea of being known by God. It opens with a declarative statement, stating simply that God has searched me and knows me. David, the psalmist, goes on to tease out what it means to be "known" by God, using verbs such as *knows*, *perceives*, and *discerns*. God knows everything, including all of David's actions, his thoughts, even his words before they leave his mouth! I would respond as David did: "Such knowledge is too wonderful for me." I don't even know myself

Know Yourself

in this intimate, all-consuming way. With poetic language, David makes the point that there simply is no place he can go and not find God. Physically, emotionally, spiritually, God knows David. Moving from the declaration at the beginning that God knows him, David ends with a plea to be searched by God, begging God to examine his heart.

This is perplexing. David has already said in the beginning of the psalm that God *knows* him and has built a strong case for the ways God indeed knows him. The difference isn't that suddenly God needed to be invited in as if David was in control of the depth of what could be known. Instead it is the difference between knowing something about people having seen them in many situations versus having them trust you with the information. You might know that they are stubborn and don't like to be given direction, but what a difference when a friend shares herself with you, demonstrating trust and vulnerability. In many ways it's like driving by a house ("Oh yeah, I know which house you're talking about") and being invited in for dinner ("Oh yeah, I know that house, my friend lives there and had me over for dinner last week").

It was during this time of moving from Chengdu to Beijing and having my community taken away that God comforted me and reassured me that He *did* know me. Yes, I was moving and there would need to be a period of rebuilding, but as Psalm 139 reminded me, it was simply not true that I was not known. It is profoundly consoling to be known deeply by One who will go with me through each season.

We looked earlier at the importance of staying grounded in Christ because doing so anchors you within the larger story, helping you avoid the temptation to turn this current chapter *into* the sum total of the story. This perspective allows for this particular season of life to come to fruition and be harvested before planting another crop in the next season. How does the farmer *know* when it's time to do these things? How does he *know* to start harvesting today instead of tomorrow or next week?

Not to sound too existential, but what does it mean to know

when to do something? For the farmer, the knowing involves science and art, facts and feeling, past and present information. In regard to facts, he knows all about his crops—how long they take to ripen and what ripeness looks like. For most people, weather forecasting has a foot in each camp with input from both weather sources (facts) and the gut/experience (feelings). The ability of the farmer to trust his gut grows over time. Why? Thanks to the beauty and mystery of knowing for himself from his own experience, he knows when to harvest, when to plant, when it's okay to take a day off. He just knows. Deeply and confidently in the inner parts of his being, he knows. He knows in the way a mother knows when there is something wrong with her baby or a student knows the minute after a test is turned in that his or her answer to a certain question was wrong. We have all had moments where we just know.

Part of finishing well involves the art and science of knowing yourself; it comes down to self-awareness. Having known yourself in many situations, there comes a point at which you will need to get real. Just as God knew King David, there are aspects you and God know about yourself, but there are parts that God can show you about yourself as you go through this transition if you, like David, invite him into the process.

This will require reflection and honesty. As God develops you throughout this transition, at times you will have insights into yourself and begin to step more fully into the man or woman he desires you to be. Other times will involve courage as you look at parts of yourself that are less attractive than you might like or that are downright ugly and in need of change. Not all of this self-discovery will be new to you. Praise be, one can only handle so much self-examination, right? Ideally, this process will not merely rehash well-trod territory but allow you to see what's changed, what's still true, and how this age or stage of life is different from previous ones.

There are four key aspects to knowing yourself that will help you finish well so that you hear from God, "Well done, good and faithful servant!" The four aspects are time management,

Know Yourself

thoroughness of task completion, grieving style, and identity. I'll present each aspect from the perspective of two categories of people. Most of you will fit nicely in either one or the other. But as you know, life is rarely neat and tidy. It's normal to identify more with one of the categories but see evidence of the other in your life as well. Don't get so hung up on the categories that you miss the point. It's not about the categories or one being the "right" way and the other being the "wrong" way to do something. Instead, how will that style or preference come into play with this phase of your life coming to an end? In what ways will your approach to each aspect of knowing yourself make life easier or more difficult for you or for others in your life? Is this transition one in which you may need to consider laying aside your preference and doing something in a different way for the sake of culture or the benefit of a relationship? Again, don't get hung up on right or wrong—instead, who is it that *you* are?

As you read the following pages, you might come across ideas you haven't thought of before and aren't sure where you fit. Transitions present opportunities to get to know yourself better. If you are going through this transition with other family members, first read this chapter with just yourself in mind. Then go back and read it again with your spouse, children, or friends in mind.

Time Management

Are you a procrastinator or someone who starts early on tasks? Now, unlike the other three aspects, this one does come with a right answer when it comes to finishing well before a transition to or from the field. Stop and hear what I'm saying. I'm not saying that one is right when it comes to life, because both have definite advantages. But when it comes to a big transition, starting early is important, so important I have devoted an entire chapter of this book to starting early. For now, simply focus on your own personality, without the fear of judgment, to determine whether you are more of a procrastinator or one who starts early.

Thoroughness of task completion

Are you a "finish the entire task" kind of person or a "doing most is good enough" kind of person? I realized two types of people exist when I bumped heads with my dad on a project, highlighting the two styles. During most of my childhood, our garage became a giant storage room as great-aunts and -uncles downsized and then passed away.[30] Many household items were put in the garage either to buy time to figure out what to do with them or to furnish future apartments my sisters and I would occupy. And the years went by. One summer, long after my sisters and I were established in homes of our own, I decided it was time to tackle the garage with the help of my sister. We discovered true treasures, such as the toys our dad had played with as a child. But other items were so random they were funny. How did we end up with a huge box full of coal? Large pieces of coal! They were so heavy that we couldn't put the box out for an unsuspecting garbage collector for fear he would throw out his back.

We worked and worked, hauling box after box into the house and getting input from Mom and Dad on what could go and what must stay. When it came down to the last box, my dad and I were working in the garage, a bit stunned that we were almost done and soon an actual car could be parked where we were standing. I was ready to dive in when Dad said, "Oh, let's just leave one box unsorted." My face left no doubt how I felt about that plan. Not finish? After having come this far?

And there on the brink of finishing, I had an epiphany. A huge light bulb went off as I understood both myself and my dad in ways moments before I couldn't have articulated. Two types of reactions emerge when it comes to the end of a momentous task: excitement and relief (me) that it's almost done or nostalgia (my dad) that brings the work to a grinding halt. Throw in some perfectionist tendencies (not in my dad's case, but I've seen it in others) for the latter personality, and it's no wonder they don't finish the job. If that's you, might I gently

Know Yourself

remind you of the importance of accepting that transitions are going to be messy.

When it comes to completing a task, are you in the "finish the entire task" category or the "doing most is good enough" category? This isn't about which one you want to be in; it's about which one you are truly in and knowing how that piece of your personality is going to play out in this transition. For those of you in the "entire task" category, you are the one others seek when things need to get done. You follow though, pure and simple, which is the upside of this orientation toward life. The downside? You tend to lose sight of the bigger picture and place a higher priority on tasks than people. The sense of a completed task is such a high for you, it's easy to discount the potential carnage left in the wake of completed tasks. As you finish, check in every so often with yourself and others to see how you are doing in this area. True, plenty needs to get done, but there are also tasks that don't need to be done to the level you might want. Are there a few tasks you can let slide?

Now, for those who believe that doing most of a job is good enough, you're right: there are times when a job doesn't need to be done all the way. What you need to do is take a look at the reason you aren't finishing certain tasks. Is it because you run out of time and need to learn to budget time better? Do you run out of finances? Do you become bored? Are you easily distracted? When a better offer comes along, do you abandon the task and move on? Are you secretly concerned about what might be expected of you if you finish, proving you are capable of more? Your tendency not to finish tasks could come from any of the above. The key is knowing yourself enough to determine why you're not a finisher.

Part of finishing well involves completing some tasks, leaving others incomplete, and knowing when to finish and when to let go. If you don't complete the tasks that have been given to you, how might that impact family, friends, and co-workers? Chances are it will impact them in ways you might not fully realize and put undue strain on relationships. Again, check in every so often with yourself and others to see how you are doing. Since relationships trump tasks, be a person who knows what to let slide and what to follow through on.

Grieving Style

Are you a pre-griever or a post-griever? The two-sided coin for relationships when you live overseas is that you get to meet a lot of wonderful people, but they rotate in and out of your life. For the most part I have been the one staying while others leave. Years ago my dear friend Anne and I were preparing to return to the U.S. at the same time and even planned to be off the field for the same amount of time: three years. Having a friend experience a parallel path was a rarity and provided an interesting and unintended emotional laboratory as Anne and I reacted differently to our upcoming return to the U.S. We both had parts of China we would miss and parts we would not miss as well as things we were looking forward to and dreading about life in the U.S. As the months went by and the upcoming move became imminent, I cried during some of our conversations while Anne never shed a tear. I'm not being dramatic in my retelling: she *never* cried before we left, which was in stark contrast to the Tissue Queen, aka me.

Anne and her family were leaving a few days before I was and had invited Wang, a Chinese friend, and me over for dinner the last night in their home. Wang and I couldn't stop the tears; I'm sure you're getting the picture that this was a really fun meal. It struck me again that Anne didn't cry. I knew she'd miss me. Well, I thought she'd miss me. I certainly hoped she would miss me. I was grieving that we would no longer be part of one another's daily lives, at least for a while. Was it too much to ask for one small tear? Just one?

And then we parted ways. I returned to Colorado, and she and her family returned to Connecticut. I had a fairly smooth transition and moved on to the next phase without too much trouble. Anne, however, had a bit of a tougher transition. This is when I first became aware of two types of grievers in the face of an impending transition: pre-grievers and post-grievers. It's not that some people don't grieve—we all do—but the timing of grief can be disarmingly different. I was a pre-griever, so by the time I left that phase of my life, I had pretty well mourned what was ending and had created (unbeknownst to me) mental and emotional space for the next phase of my life. Anne, on the other hand, is a post-griever. Her grieving process didn't start until she had the challenge of mourning China in Connecticut, surrounded by people who were happy to be with her and her family, which is not as easy as you might think.

Both personality wirings have beneficial aspects that make the other type jealous, as well as some real downsides. Pre-grievers are able to say goodbye to people and places in person and are able to move on to the next thing. It makes sense to those around them why they are grieving; the onlookers to the process knowingly nod, hand a tissue, and privately think to themselves, "You will be leaving soon, and you will miss me so much. Of course, you're sad. Who wouldn't be?" One downside, however, is that for others close to pre-grievers, the last weeks and months are more of an emotional roller coaster, involving tears and emotional upheavals.

On the other hand, because post-grievers don't start the grieving process until after a change has occurred, they get to end the phase more emotionally together. One benefit of being a post-griever is the ability to focus and get things done. The downside, however, is that when they enter the grieving process, they are often surrounded by people who don't fully understand what is being grieved.

You can see how this can add to the messiness when a pre-griever is married to or friends with a post-griever. My friends Sam and Patty were preparing to send their first child off to college, but each responded differently to the upcoming transition in their family. Understanding that Sam is a pre-griever and Patty a post-griever helped them to make sense of their different reactions. It wasn't that Patty wouldn't miss their daughter Sara or that Sam was having trouble letting her go or that either one of them was "wrong" in the way they were grieving. It can simply get complicated when spouses' or friends' grieving cycles are more than a little bit off. As with other personality types mentioned, it will be tempting to judge the other style. *You don't care as much as I do! Can't you show a little emotion? Why can't you hold it together more? How can you pack up our whole life so calmly? Why can't you do anything without talking about how much you'll miss this or that?*

Rarely is someone wholly a pre-griever or a post-griever; most have strong leanings mixed with forays into the other style. As you look back over transitions you have gone through in your life, what memories float to the surface pointing to one grieving style or the other? I now understand why I was a basket case the last day of school every year. I sobbed like a fool in the girl's bathroom with other pre-grievers. What were we going to do with those long, boring summer days, and who wouldn't want to stay in fourth grade forever?! Yes, part of this was pre-adolescent girl drama; however, because I am a pre-griever, the next day I was up and at 'em, filling my days with the wonders of summer vacation. I also recall my mom walking in on me crying one day, wondering what was wrong with me. I was just thinking about how sad I would be when my cat Patches would die . . . many years in the future, it turned out. These were clear signs of being a pre-griever long before I could even name, let alone explain, what was going on.

Likewise, there are probably experiences you've had that point to you being a pre-or post-griever. Thinking back, are you more prone to distance yourself from those close to you before a transition or after it? Do you cry, become short, or feel paralyzed before or after an event? Knowing this about yourself will help you to make sense of the way you and those near you express what is happening. For pre-grievers it's helpful to know that just because people aren't expressing their grief or sadness, it doesn't mean their time, experience, or relationship with you is unimportant. And for post-grievers, it's important for you to remember that pre-grievers aren't emotional basket cases; your time will come.

Identity

The final area we will look at in this section involves your identity and who you are apart from this life transition. In times of transition, parts of your identity can become disproportionately large as you seek to find significance and a sense of anchoring in a sea of change. The Sirens will call out to you, tempting you to grasp on to one part of who you are and whisper how *that* aspect is really the sole aspect of who you are. They will lie and say that you are *nothing* apart from this part of you. While this part of you—this role, job, location—certainly can be a significant part of you, it must not become the only part. If this concept doesn't stay in the forefront of your thoughts and conversations, it can leave you on the other side of the transition wondering *who am I* when this defining aspect is now gone or profoundly changed. *Who am I . . .*

- when I have to ask others to financially support me or my family?
- when I can't speak the language?
- when I have to be a home schooling mom because there are no other viable education options?
- when what made me unique is taken away (when I don't live overseas, have that job, live in the interesting place)?
- when I experience a shift in responsibilities, power, or influence?

This area of identity cuts to the heart in ways that time management, thoroughness of task completion, and grieving style simply don't. You can be a post-griever without it saying anything about your value as a person. You can be a son, daughter, father, or mother without it being too largely impacted by whether you complete or partially complete tasks. But what does it mean to be a daughter when you are moving to the other side of the world and won't be able to help with family emergencies?

I wrote the following as a blog post about five months after the largest transition of my life: having quit my job in China and moved back to the U.S. The comments, emails, Facebook messages, and texts flooded in, showing I'm not alone in these wonderings.

> I am standing witness to my story. When the idea first started to tug at my soul, I resisted it. Too afraid and overwhelmed of what it might mean. What it might cost me. What it would require me to examine. I pushed it down.
>
> Down.
>
> Down.
>
> Down.
>
> But when something's being born in you, you can only shove it down so many times.
>
> *Is it time to leave this organization? This company I love?* I couldn't yet consider leaving China. China had become so intertwined with my identity, it became the most prominent adjective describing me. *Oh, you're the China daughter. The aunt who lives in China. The college friend in China. The foreign teacher in China. The sister in China.* What word is used over and over and over? Not daughter, aunt, friend, teacher, or sister.
>
> China.
>
> This is my greatest fear. What if China is what makes me and the story of my life interesting and without her I'm dull? I fear that I may not matter and people only listened to me because I was a bit exotic. If you're like me, this is the part where you want to rush in to interrupt and say, "No, no, YOU are interesting. I like you. China, sure,

Know Yourself

she's nice too." But don't we all wonder? What makes our story enticing to others? What draws people to us?

Once we've been in a certain plot line long enough, sorting through strands can be a bit like untangling a messy ball of yarn. How much do our jobs, our roles, our families define us?

We are made to be communal. To ebb and flow. Of course our jobs, our locations, our children are going to leave their marks on us, like waves hitting the beaches. They will change the contours of our souls' shorelines. But don't you at times wonder who you are? Really are?

Like Jacob, I wrestled. If only it had been for one night and not long and hard! I wrestled with my calling, the nature and longevity of it, as well as with my identity. When you've thrown your lot in so long with a place and a people and loyalty is also your story, what does it mean to move on? To outgrow? To hear other whispers? Was I willing to stay in a story I thought was interesting on the surface so that people would think I am interesting even though I was fading in it? Was I the kind of person who cared so much about others' opinions I was willing to prostitute myself to be interesting? Was being interesting my altar?

I, too, now walk with a limp. It's metaphorical and I don't show it all that often. But my identity has taken a hit. I feel like a mom whose last child has flown the nest. But I have no children to point to. Instead I'm the one who has flown. And a part of me will always be China Amy. The daughter, sister, friend, aunt who lived in China.

Now I'm having to find out who I am without China in my daily life. The story will continue, but the plot isn't as predictable as it was. There is comfort in predictability, isn't there? Parts of this new phase are exciting. I needed a change. But fear is here, too. And loss. What will become the new defining adjective? How long will it take? What if I really am boring? It is tempting to rush through this in-between phase of life and hurry on to the next thing. Yet there is much life to be lived here, too, in the in-between phase.

I'm too close to it to see clearly. But I am far enough into this identity-changing process to be glad I listened to the voice that wouldn't let me go instead of clinging to my idea of who I am.

Fun facts or core to who you are?

Many questions will be stirred up in you during your time of transition. In terms of knowing yourself, it's important to acknowledge the roles you have played and the ways they will change as you enter the transition. The key is how much you define yourself by this role. One way to get a quick read is to ask yourself this: on a scale of one to ten, how much would I still be me if _____ was taken away? While there are many parts that help identify who we are, they don't all define us to the same degree. Ranking different parts can help to sort out which are fun facts (like having a favorite sports team or liking to eat scorpions) to others that would radically change who you are or how you invest your time.

Knowing how much your identity is intertwined with what is coming to an end will help make sense of the different reactions you and others are having. It won't (nor shouldn't) necessarily change your reactions; it's more about informing. It also helps to begin to think of what will define you both now and after the transition. The challenge will be to focus on character aspects instead of roles. Roles may change, but character traits carry over. If you find yourself more strongly clinging to a role than to a character aspect in times of transition, you may need to repeat to yourself a phrase John the Baptist used regarding Jesus and himself. He simply said, "He must increase, I must decrease."[31] So it is in times of transition. For your identity, "Character must increase; roles must decrease."

To break this process down into practical steps, think through

Know Yourself

some of the roles you have and the ways each role taps into who you are beyond the label. On the left-hand side of a piece of paper, write down your different roles. On the right hand-side, list ways that they have impacted who you are as a person. For example, if you have lived overseas, you are more than "just" someone who can live outside of your home culture; you are now flexible in ways you couldn't have been without that experience. So the left side would list "cross-cultural worker/resident" and the right would mention flexibility. Or the ways that being a parent (left-hand column) grows patience in a person (right-hand column). Flexibility and patience will outlive the primary roles that they were developed in. If you continue to cling to a role without allowing it to change, there will come a point at which the role no longer serves you, but you serve the role. You will become someone whose best days are behind you as you orient yourself to a reality that has passed. That's why this is the most significant and in many ways hardest aspect of knowing yourself. Having an identity is good and healthy. However, not allowing what defines us to change causes stagnation. Acknowledging where your identity comes from and ultimately building on things that will outlast this transition will help you to finish this leg of your journey well.

One final word on identity: in some cases what is being lost or changed pales in comparison to what is being gained. Relocating due to a promotion, being assigned to a new field because of your unique training, actually preparing to go to the field and not just talking about it, and returning home to start grad school are easier to identify as being positive. But in other cases, the role a person is moving toward is one that involves great loss. And so we circle back to the messiness of looming transitions and the importance of staying grounded in Christ.

The importance of knowing yourself

If the road to hell is paved with good intentions, the road to finishing a transition poorly is to assume everyone must walk down the road in the same way. It's tempting to try to calm the chaos of life with oversimplified platitudes, while tidy lists trick you into believing that if you follow them, you will easily arrive at the desired destination. Life's messiness can be exhausting, and if a much simpler way is offered, why not take it? The truth is that many pop psychology and self-help books represent real life in the way that fool's gold represents real gold. Part of knowing yourself is walking into the messiness of transition with open eyes and being able to say, "This is how I am wired and this is how it might influence others."

Given the four areas we have examined—time management, thoroughness of task completion, grieving style, and identity—can you imagine all of the potential combinations within a person? Even within the same home, a post-grieving task completer will probably go down a path more freely and quickly than someone who waits until the last minute and is having his or her identity shaken. But if spouses, friends, family members all know themselves (and each other), it will allow for give-and-take as one may need more space and grace in certain areas and less in others. If you can, share with others what you know to be true about yourself. It's not something you need to excuse or even to change, but the more you know about yourself, the more you are able to work from your strengths instead of from your weaknesses.

The ebb and flow of what it means to be known in Psalm 139 shows the paradox of knowing. The more you know and understand yourself, the more you see how wonderfully and fearfully made you are and that there is far more to know than you realized. Hopefully this will lead you, like David, to open yourself to *be searched* by God during this transition so that you might grow through it, finish well, and ultimately hear the One who truly knows you say, "Well done!"

Chapter 7

Start Early

It is only the farmer who faithfully plants seeds in the Spring, who reaps a harvest in the Autumn.
—BC Forbes

In recent years my sister has been lovingly encouraging our parents to start going through their possessions so they can see what's worth keeping and what should be given away. The impetus behind the campaign is twofold. One, my sister is not a saver. Purging stuff makes her feel good, like a natural high. If she's beginning to feel overwhelmed with life, a good round of reducing things from her house is like the wind beneath her wings. Not so for our parents, ergo a little bit of the resistance. Since they refer to their things as "old friends," you can bet that this isn't going to be a life-giving exercise for them. However, the real impetus behind her encouragement is that she has had to help move her in-laws a couple of times. It doesn't take a rocket scientist to discover, after packing up the same things multiple times, that you either deal with it now or you deal with it later.

In a cartoon about the early bird getting the worm, one bird says to the other, "I got up at 5:30 a.m. once and caught a worm. It wasn't worth it, trust me." Chuckle, chuckle. We chuckle (or roll our eyes) because, as mentioned in the chapter on laughter, the punch line touches something deeper: the question of worth. Is it really worth getting off your duff and getting something done? Don't we fear that our efforts won't be worth it? And if this transition was just about the physical stuff in your life, a case could be made for either side: starting early or waiting until the last minute. But it's not simply about material things. It is about more than just moving something from point A to point B; it's about bringing one chapter in life to a close so you can turn a page to the next.

Of all the areas examined in this book, this one—starting early—will be the most prescriptive. I believe the majority of us face events in life with the best of intentions and desires for a positive outcome. Unfortunately, without a structure to support the plan, our intentions become like wet concrete poured out over dirt. Yes, some will end up where it's intended to go, but without a form to pour the concrete into, most of it will end up wherever the path of least resistance leads it. There comes a certain point at which it is too late. That which was fluid before has become solid and is now out of all options but the most drastic (e.g., using a jackhammer). By starting early, you are able to create the forms that allow you to pour the concrete where you'd like, leading to fewer regrets and a stronger finish. If you start preparing for your transition early, you can invest in areas that are important to you instead of reacting as they come up.

It's about both

I've used the analogy that fertile souls are like fertile fields as they both hold stories with multiple chapters. And while the story isn't merely about this one crop, or transition, the current chapter of the story most certainly is. The point of starting early isn't to have everything done super early so you are sitting in an empty office, dorm room, or home; the point is for you to have time to incorporate all parts of your life into the plan, ensuring that you are living out of your priorities. Just as the farmer has to live within the rhythm of a growth cycle and must wait for certain events to occur before the next step can be taken, starting early will involve pacing and patience. As the farmer needs the ability to adapt to the weather, making plans but adjusting to the current winds and rain, so you too will need the ability to adapt

Start Early

to the unpredictable. This makes finishing well about both the macro and the micro story. One is not more important than the other; in fact, without both of them, neither exists.

Starting early boils down to having a game plan. The best coaches don't just show up for a game and hope for the best. They have a plan and have worked out ahead of time a number of scenarios so they are better able to adapt in the moment to what the other team presents. For some people, it is hard to make a plan when it comes to their lives. It feels too daunting and constraining, and the amount of follow-through it requires exhausts them even before they've started. For others, the challenge is flexing when the plan needs to change. Both approaches give a plan too much power and control. If handled well, a plan provides structure while allowing for the messiness of things that come up in transitions.

To create your plan, list all of the things that you'd like to accomplish between now and the end of this leg of your journey. Using a master calendar, plug in all of the tasks on your list. Voila, it's that simple. Next chapter.

Well, probably not. You know it's not that simple. The rest of this chapter will be interactive, so you'll want to use a notebook of some sort. In your notebook make a list of everything you need to do and want to see happen in the upcoming months. Next we will transform your list into a plan. Start by dividing your list according to the following four categories: (1) paperwork, (2) personal belongings, (3) people, and (4) places and experiences.

Paperwork

In this section we will look at five types of paperwork you might need to complete for your upcoming transition:
- Applications
- Legal considerations
- Job-related
- Reservations or bookings
- Financial considerations

Looming Transitions

As you read through the list, did you find yourself thinking of the game show *Jeopardy*? I could almost hear Alex Trebek reading the categories, and I want to respond, "I'll take 'job-related' for two-hundred dollars, Alex." While some of the things you're going to need to do might feel like being in actual jeopardy, use the following as a guide to think through the paperwork that will need to be completed. Not every one of these areas will apply to your situation, and there will certainly be other ones that haven't been included; feel free to skip what is not relevant, and add to the list other paperwork requirements as they come to mind.

Applications: What applications do you need to complete? Be sure to know what information and documentation you will need. List the items that you will need to procure ahead of time, such as photographs, marriage certificates, birth certificates, diplomas or transcripts, contact information, and financial documents. Whom do you need to notify because you will need their help? If you're processing a visa, do you need to authenticate any of your paperwork? If you have no idea what I'm talking about, be glad.

Legal considerations: Do you have a power of attorney? If not, do you need one? Do you have a current will? Do you or your loved ones want or need a DNR (do not resuscitate) order? Do people who will be making decisions in case of your death know whether or not you are an organ donor? Have you looked into funeral arrangements? If not, do you need to consider this? If you have children, do you have legal guardians appointed in case of your death? This area of legal considerations is often an area we know we *should* get around to, but in the busyness of life it often gets shoved aside.

Sadly a death of a family member who does not have a will can add legal complications, resulting in unanticipated headache. This point was brought home to me when a healthy man from our church in Denver dropped dead on the tennis court.

Start Early

He was from India, and because he was young and healthy, his legal affairs in the U.S. weren't in order. This meant his wife and daughter were not able to travel to India to grieve with their extended family. Seeing the unintended stress this caused his family, I decided soon after to arrange my will and medical documents out of consideration for my family. In times of crisis, the best way to ensure you can be in whatever country you want is to have as much in place as possible *before* it is ever needed.

Does someone know where your legal documents are kept and whom to contact in case of an emergency? Are there any documents that will need a notary public or verification of some kind? This is a service U.S. embassies around the world provide for a fee. Check what legal services your country provides.

Job-related: If you are moving to another job, what procedures and documentation do you need to leave for your successor? Part of finishing well is handing off well. Are there any handbooks that need to be updated? What are the tasks that primarily you do around the office that you need to train someone else to do? For example, do you have the magic touch with the copy machine? Are you the only one who knows how to make coffee or use the fax machine? Think beyond just the obvious of your job description. The degree of detail in job-related tasks may vary depending on whether you are staying with the organization and merely relocating or changing jobs completely.

Reservations or Bookings: What other bookings or arrangements do you need to make? These might include airline tickets, storage units, moving vans, doctor appointments, or child care. If a vacation is being planned before your actual transition, what needs to be arranged and do people know their responsibilities while you're gone?

Financial considerations: We briefly touched on finances when we talked about the messiness of transitions. What are the financial considerations for this transition? Do you need to travel to visit supporters? Are there places you or your family wants or needs to visit? Are you transitioning a child off to college either prior to leaving for the field or soon after you make this transition? Will you need a vehicle or housing in the months leading up to and then after the transition? What costs are involved in shipping or in taking extra luggage?

Of the four categories in your plan (paperwork, personal belongings, people, and places and experiences), paperwork is the one that is most likely to get your attention because you can't move forward without attending to it. Tasks are concrete and easier to measure as to whether or not they were tended to; it's much simpler to answer, "Did you book the tickets?" than "Did you have enough time with the people whom you wanted to meet with before you left?" Indeed, paperwork *does* need to be tended to but not at the expense of the other areas. Finishing well involves more than just a list of completed tasks. For those who are more task-oriented, it's fine to turn the other areas into tasks as long as the people you interact with don't feel like you're merely checking them off a list. And for those who are more relational and the above list of questions has you depressed, look for ways to accomplish the tasks alongside friends and family.

Personal Belongings

This is also an area that was touched on earlier when we looked at things that can get messy. I heard yesterday that sixteen of the thirty-eight parables in the New Testament deal with possessions and money.[32] Possessions were a big deal back then, no surprise they are going to be a big deal now. For those who are like my sister, this is a wonderful time to move items on to new homes. It is a lightening of the load. But for those of you who view your possessions as "old friends," this is an area where you can become overwhelmed and bogged down. It can be a deep source of grief. If this is you, instead of just jumping in, do some mental pre-work. Have a discussion with your spouse, or roommate to see if you are operating from the same assumptions about the amount you will take and the timing of selling

Start Early

and giving away. If you lived communally overseas you know how often items can be a huge source of hidden assumptions. Take time to work through your priorities and how you will make decisions about your belongings. This is one of the reasons to start early, so that you have time to think through how you want to approach all of the decisions that need to be made.

- Use the following six categories to begin to organize your belongings: *sell, give away, throw away, store, buy*[33] and *move*.
- Categorize the belongings you plan to store or move with you: furniture, toiletries, bedding/linens, kitchen supplies, books, entertainment equipment, office supplies, clothing, toys, and decorations.
- We all have comfort objects, items we treasure regardless of where we live or where we move. While transition objects are most commonly associated with young children, aiding them at bedtime or in a parent's absence, more recently research on the elderly has found that older people benefit from transition objects as well.[34] I believe it's not just children and the elderly who benefit from transition objects; we all do. I found that when I returned to the U.S. for a three year study leave, I "really needed" almost all of my picture frames because they documented places I had been, my friends, and my family. So I boxed them up and mailed them to Colorado. It brought me great comfort knowing I would always have my pictures if for some reason I was never able to return to China. I did open the box during my U.S. stay, but I never really unpacked them, and three years later I resealed the box and mailed them back to China. Some might view this as a colossal waste of money. But in my view, the psychological comfort that one box provided far outweighed the cost. Notice that it was one box and is called a transition *object* and not objects (plural).[35] For some people narrowing down comforting transition objects will be challenging. While one person in your family may only need one or two transition objects,

Looming Transitions

you may need five or six. If the amount becomes excessive, realize that you cannot recreate your current life in a post-transition one. Creating the space for things to die so that new things can be born involves just that—creating space.

If you have kids, talk with them about transition objects and, if age appropriate, allow them to pick what they would like to take with them. Beth, a friend who read a draft of this book as she and her family prepared to leave the field, shared the following after reading this section:

> With the kids, there would be only so many toys and books that we could reasonably take with us. Early on, like six months before departure date, I rearranged their room (they share a room) and put shelves in. I told them to select all the toys they wanted to be sure to take with them when we moved and put them on the shelves. They did a good job at figuring out what they wanted to take. Over the following months they pared that down a little themselves, as they figured that they really were done with something, or that they wanted to give a friend a particular toy. The other toys not on the shelves were in another part of the apartment. They took time over the last several months to still play with them, but with the idea that the time would end at some point. Totally their decision. And boy, has it made it easier now that we are at the place of actually putting things in action packers to see what fits. No sudden goodbyes to beloved toys! Starting early has paid off.
>
> We did the same with their books. Separated the ones to take and the ones to give away, but did it months ahead do they could add a few to take with us if they changed their mind. And they have still gone to the giveaway pile and pulled books to read at bedtime and put them back afterwards, remembering that they are not going to take

Start Early

it, but can still enjoy it now. So, they have been "saying goodbye" to their books over a period of time—starting early with this has indeed helped make it a bit more . . . hmm . . . dare I say easier to part with much loved books and toys.

People

This area might require the most intentionality because it's easier to cancel on a lunch date than the movers coming. In the grand scheme of things, it's the time with people that is equally important as, if not more important than, the paperwork and personal belongings that need to be dealt with. Part of finishing well involves making sure the urgency of tasks doesn't take precedence over the life-giving relationships you need to nurture. As you think through the people you want to connect with before this transition, there are several ways to group them:

- Who are the people your family wants to spend time with? (groups)
- Who are the couples that you and your spouse want to spend time with? (couples)
- Who is it that you want to be sure that you or your children have some time with? (individuals)

The next piece to think through is the type of interaction that you want with loved ones before your transition. Will a one-time event (e.g., a picnic) suffice, or does it need to be larger (e.g., a weekend camping trip)? Will a phone call be sufficient? A meal? Is there anyone that you need to travel to visit? Who are the people you will miss seeing but don't need to really do anything about it, other than acknowledge to yourself you will miss them? An example of this type of person might be a checkout person at the local grocery store or an instructor at the local gym. One of the benefits of transitions is reflection on how many good people are in your life.

One of the final things to think about when it comes to people

Looming Transitions

is how often you need or want to see them in the time building up to the transition. There will be some people with whom once is enough and others whom you will want to see multiple times. It's amazing how many people can come out of the woodwork in the last week or two before a big transition. Often they have known for months about this change, but suddenly they just *have* to see you.

Remember that while all people are equal, not so all relationships. As the clock winds down for you, it is okay to rank and give priority to those closer and more important to you. If you don't, you might find yourself spending precious time with those who really aren't as important to you as others. If this is difficult for you, think in advance about how you want to handle requests so that you show value to people but do not obligate yourself to commitments you would rather not invest in. One basic rule is to buy yourself time to decide. Often we agree to activities or meetings we later regret because we said yes too quickly. A great stock line is "Let me check my schedule and get back with you." Depending on the situation and your personality, you might enlist a friend who would be willing to coordinate your schedule, either for organizational reasons or for your friend to be the heavy and say no to some people.

If it won't work out to meet with someone, you don't owe them a big explanation as to why. A simple "It's not going to work out, but I really appreciate the thought!" will suffice. I can already hear a few of you because this may seem to be nearly a heretical thought: *What?! I can't NOT give an explanation.* Actually, you can. If you sense yourself wanting to give a long explanation, it might say more about you and your desire to please others. I'm not saying you should feel prohibited from giving one. There are some situations where the right thing to do is to give an explanation; the point is that you don't have to meet with someone just because they asked. Not all relationships are equal, so it's not necessary to treat them as if they are; some you owe an explanation, others just a clear answer so they aren't left wondering if you are meeting or not. This might be new cultural

Start Early

territory. If you're not sure how to navigate the no's you'll need to give in your cultural context, ask a local friend. I sometimes forget in these situations that I don't have to know everything, and neither do you. It is helpful to have a plan before you'll need it.

Places and Experiences

In the 1960s, Charles Hummel wrote a pamphlet that helped draw a line in the sand between urgent and important. Aptly titled *Tyranny of the Urgent,* he argues that in the tension between the urgent and the important, far too often the urgent wins.[36] Although places you want to visit and experiences you want to have before this leg of the journey comes to an end is being looked at last, it might be the most important. Visiting places and having certain experiences are the most likely to get squeezed out of your schedule because they may not appear urgent compared to other tasks. Right now, while you are thinking about it, what are the favorite places you want to visit at least "one more time"—or maybe multiple times—before you go? List anything that comes to mind in the following categories:

- Favorite or special restaurants, coffee shops, or tea houses
- Stores
- Places you regularly visit (the library, a movie theater, the zoo, a park, botanic gardens, the gym, a campus, a street)
- Activities you regularly participate in (a bible study or small group, walking with a friend, a gym class, a book club, a civic group, a TV show you watch regularly with a group, sport teams you play for or watch with others, outdoor activities such as hiking or skiing)
- Other places you've always meant to visit but just haven't yet

Obviously some places and experiences on this list are naturally paired with people. Don't get bogged down in the overlapping of the categories. If you have been living a rich and full life, your list of people, places, and experiences is probably fairly long. Just as all relationships aren't equal, everything you're involved in isn't equal; look over your list and group things into three categories:

1. If I don't visit here at least one more time, I'll regret it for the rest of my life.
2. I'd really like to do this, but if something has to give, this could be something that I let go.
3. In the grand scheme of things, my memories are good enough.

As you are making decisions in the next months, keep these in mind. Every now and then revisit your list (even if just mentally) to check if your values and priorities are reflected in your decisions and the ways you are investing your time. A battle cry for this season is start early, eat often. As you near your time of transition, don't put off enjoying spending time with people in some of your favorite places doing some of your favorite activities.

Not just for squeaky wheels

If these four areas—paperwork, personal belongings, people, places and experiences—were wheels on a wagon that represents your life, paperwork would be the squeakiest wheel. While the saying is that the squeaky wheel gets the grease, it may not be the only wheel that needs it. Part of finishing well is finishing well in *all* areas and not merely finishing. Does it take effort and intentionality to finish well? You bet. Is it worth it? Absolutely. That doesn't mean there won't be frustrations, disagreements, and hard decisions, but in the end finishing well means you can look back with few regrets and little collateral damage. Do not get yourself backed into a corner because you didn't start early enough that you can only react to the squeaky wheel; all four wheels are necessary to move the wagon. Investing time in making a plan will pay off.

Start Early

Where to go from here?

Whether you have sat down and written answers to all of the questions in this chapter so far or simply read through them and plan to go back later, you might have one of two primary reactions. The thought of all that needs to be done can be utterly overwhelming, leading some readers just to keep on reading and put this entire chapter out of their minds. For others, there is no time like the present; they want to get as much done as possible RIGHT NOW.

As with other areas, welcome to the tension of needing to get started but not being able to get everything done until the very end (and even then you'll have things waiting for you on the other side of your transition). The plan of attack you will formulate needs to be in conjunction with your personality and the way you process, organize, and store information and whether you use some form of technology or paper and pencil. While some people will have strong preferences about the best way to go about a plan of attack, the best way is going to be the one that works for you. I have bought several devices intended to radically help my life. And they would have if I had ever used them. Give me lists on paper and a calendar I can write on and I am good to go. Is this better than using some sort of electronic device? It is better only in that it works for me. As we look at ways to organize the tasks you need to accomplish, the people you want to see, and the places you want to visit, know what will work for you and then use that system for all it's worth.

Next question: is it time sensitive or not?

The next step in the process is to sort everything on your lists according to those items that are time sensitive and those that are not time sensitive. Either you can use a T for "Time Sensitive" or an N for "Not Time Sensitive" or you can make a chart— whatever works for you. Time sensitive might involve significant birthdays or anniversaries, application deadlines, sporting events, seasonal activities (like apple picking, camping, or attending a holiday festival), or activities related to school or work rhythms. As you move on to the next step of placing things on a calendar or time line, you are probably looking at four months to a year of advanced planning.

Because time-sensitive activities are tied to a calendar, it is important to treat them as the "big rocks" and put them in first, allowing for the events that are not tied to the calendar to fill in around them. It will also be helpful to come up with some kind of coding among list items, showing which can be let go, if needed, and which are essential (this will be true for both the T and the N items). There will be times when your schedule is overloaded, and you will have to make hard choices. Under pressure, it can be overwhelming to decide what to cut out. Plotting your calendar carefully ahead of time will help you to think more clearly in those high-pressure times when life feels overwhelming.

The majority of your list will probably not be time sensitive, leaving most of the scheduling work to be done according to your own priorities. As you look over your list, begin to pencil in general ideas or goals for each month approaching your transition; try to have representatives from each of the four categories if possible. While you might not be able to nail down a dinner date with a friend five months in advance, it is reasonable to have dinner with the Smiths listed under "goals/plans for September." Before each new month starts, look over your plans for that particular month and the events that you need to arrange. There will also be items on your list (for example, "go through bathroom closet") that are easy to keep putting off. Schedule them on a particular evening or weekend day. If something comes up that you want to participate in, it is okay to reschedule, but that's what you'll need to do: reschedule that non-time-sensitive event (not just cancel it).

If this all sounds a little programmatic to you, let's briefly review the thinking behind starting early. This transition is going to have your fingerprints and influence all over it. Starting early doesn't remove the unique approaches and challenges you

Start Early

will bring to it. Instead, starting early frees you up to be your best you. Now, if you are a notorious procrastinator to the point that *being you* is linked with being last-minute, you might wonder how this approach will enhance your you-ness. You have a choice.

Procrastinating may be your preference, but that's what it is, a preference. It's not a birthright. In the wagon of life, all four wheels—paperwork, personal belongings, people, places and experiences—are all needed to move the wagon from one place to another. If you procrastinate, you simply will not have time for each of these areas and the potential for finishing well will be jeopardized. You'll finish, surely. And your stuff will get moved from point A to point B. But there will be things you will inevitably miss out on. Can I tell you what they are? Not specifically, no. But in principle, yes. You will miss out on conversations and experiences that you will never fully know, although there will be hints in the months after this time is past. You will miss out on opportunities to reflect on the different people you have met and ways to mark and celebrate their influence on your life. You will miss out on ways to sort through your possessions and make mindful decisions instead of reactionary ones. You will miss out. And this won't come with a do-over option later. Oh, you'll finish, just not well. However, starting early allows for conversations, connections, gratitude, reflection, and celebration. Starting early is a gift you give yourself, your family, and your community. Starting early is a gift that can be cherished for years.

Chapter 8

It's Not Just About You

Life becomes harder for us when we live for others, but it also becomes richer and happier.
—Albert Schweitzer

My recent transition back to the States was difficult for the community I had been a part of in Beijing. In addition to my resignation from the organization I had been a part of for nearly two decades, two other families were leaving as well. Matt and Sally had met in China, fallen in love, gotten married, and had two daughters. I knew Sally when she first came to China as a college student and served in a town about an hour away from where I lived. Mike and Anne (my post-griever friend about whom I wondered, "Can you please shed a tear?" before her return to the U.S.) had come to China with two kids and were leaving with four. Their daughter, who was a preschooler when I met her, was going to college. College! Where had the time gone? All to say, this was a fairly significant time for our community. In preparation for a goodbye party a few weeks before we left, we were asked to email photos of ourselves, "fun" stories, and truths and lies. In response to the request, I wrote a semi-snarky reply:

> I've sent photos—have more stuck in my outbox for you, thank you Internet. Smiley face.
> The stories are hard. Over the years I've told all the stories I want to tell—I'm not shy about talking about my-

It's Not Just About You

self, as we know. Smiley face.

The stories that mean the most to me probably aren't good for the party atmosphere—they are about deep heart stuff.

OK, fluffy stories: Um.

1. I had to kill two mice to get to the toilet one morning.

2. Three truths and a lie (you decide): I've been woken up by a mouse running across my face. I've been woken up because the room next to me was on fire. I've been woken up with the news a family member was in the hospital. I've been woken up by someone borrowing eggs out of my refrigerator.

3. I once kissed Stan Farling over the phone.[37]

Sorry I'm not more into this . . . I feel like I've been telling stories all year and am tired of hearing myself talk about me. I'm ready for a more interesting topic!

—Amy

If you're wondering how this email from a worn-out goodbyer ties in with the title of this chapter, stick with me. My parents have an out-of-control mint garden in their backyard. While the taste and smell of fresh mint are a delight in summer, its ability to overrun other plants—though impressive—is not. One July I decided to tackle "the mighty mint" and tame it back to the original corner of the garden from whence it came. Naively I thought this would be a simple weeding project. Much to my chagrin, I discovered I had met my match. I would pull up a plant only to discover its roots led me, at times, to a nearby plant and, other times, a surprisingly far distance. I'd pull up a plant only to be off again chasing the roots to the next nuisance. Needless to say, I never came to a mint plant that wasn't connected to another one.

As I grumbled to myself around the garden, as hard as it was to believe, the truth remained: all the mint I saw started with one simple plant years before. However, with the apparently optimal conditions for growth, it sure hadn't stayed its singular self. Plants that didn't look to have any relation to one another above ground were integrally related mere inches below the surface. You are the mint plant. Delightful. Impressive. And far more connected to others than might be casually obvious.

Returning to my semi-snarky email, in hindsight I'm a bit embarrassed I didn't respond more graciously to a teammate tasked with gathering stories for a party that was supposed to be fun. Your goodbyes may have been going on as long as mine had—by that point for months. I exaggerated in my email out of annoyance and exhaustion. But my transition was not just about me.

Years ago I heard a comparison between the workings of a team and a mobile hanging above a baby's crib. The mobile consists of stand-alone parts that make up the whole. If you tug on the lion, the whole mobile will move. But it's not the only animal moving. Though the giraffe wasn't touched, it will feel the effect and move too. Likewise in times of change, you might be the person predominantly going through the transition to or from the field, but you are not the only one to feel the impact. Others will be jostled simply because they are connected to you. This is what it means to be connected to others. Whether or not you want to impact their lives, you will.

The unpredictable reality is that no neat formula exists to predict how much someone is going to be jiggled by what is going on in your life. As with the mint plants, where I couldn't tell if the roots were going to lead me to a nearby plant or one in a different part of the garden, so too with others in our lives; the degree to which they feel your change will not necessarily make logical sense. Some you expect to be deeply jostled end up only slightly jostled. And then others, well now, you won't see their reactions coming.

The word *slightly* is not meant to diminish the impact you have had on their lives or theirs on yours; it's just that reactions vary. It is tempting to measure how much you have meant to someone by the size of their reaction to your departure, but this reduces relationships to a scorecard. 1 Corinthians 13 is about as clear as you can get when it comes to love and scorekeeping: don't do it. You matter, others matter; how this is expressed shouldn't be the gauge of how much.

Part of finishing well is living with the tension that you are not the only one having something end. Again, it's not just about you. This truth involves making conscious choices that allow others to finish well with you. Due to the stress associated with transitions, this area is ripe for extremes. You may swing to the side of always saying yes in an effort to please everyone and not miss out on anything, which often leads to exhaustion and resentment. Yet swinging to the other extreme takes into account only your concerns and needs, leading to exclusion of those closest to you; this path focuses too much on you and not enough on others. Your default must not become one extreme or the other. There will be times when it is necessary to say no to people or invitations, but other times the right thing will involve choices you find to be emotionally draining.

Let's revisit Donald Miller's phrase *keeping your soul fertile*, which requires allowing space to be created through death. Earlier I said souls are like fields, and part of this is because they can be cultivated and nurtured or neglected and ignored. Ultimately a farmer wants to care for his fields so that they will be able to produce a crop. Farming is different from dabbling in gardening because the farmer's goal is to feed more than himself—for him, fertility is gauged by the ability to feed many through his efforts. The fruit of your life is seen, in part, through the relationships you have. This is another reason to start early: you will be working not only with what *you* need and *your* time frame but with those of others as well. You are to be a conduit of blessing to others, and in times of transition, part of that translates into actively participating in *their* finishing well.

The focus of attention

As the clock ticks toward your transition and the end becomes more and more a reality, those around you will want to find ways to share with you the difference you've made. Allowing others to finish in ways that are meaningful for them will be directly impacted by two areas: personality and pain.

We've already talked about the importance of knowing yourself—it comes to bear here as well. Let me ask a question about your personality. Are you more likely to be the life of the party, smack dab in the center of the action, or the one who enjoys the party but stays in the background? Probably the look on your face as you read that question spoke volumes. If your personality makes you more comfortable in the center of the action, the thought of helping others to finish well will be less draining for you because it's not a new role; however, if you are more a behind-the-scenes kind of person, being the center of attention is exhausting anytime, and even more so during life transitions.

A friend who returned to the States after years in China wanted to walk out the door one day with her suitcases and fly away without any special notice. She was a private person, and while she loved being with people, she didn't want to inconvenience anyone, even though she had been an active part of our community. If the transition had just been about her, she could have approached it any way that worked for her. But since she was leaving a big hole (in a good way . . . how much sadder if someone left after nine years with anyone hardly noticing), it was no longer just about her. Personality will factor in—and hopefully those planning goodbye events will factor this in as well—but it's not a free pass. There will be times for you to go outside of your comfort zone.

Personality isn't the only factor when it comes to allowing others to finish well; there's also the amount of pain you will experience. It's often not just one goodbye; it may be goodbye after goodbye after goodbye. In writing you're not supposed to repeat a word or phrase to the extent I did in the previous sentence, but moving from one country or location to another is a goodbye gauntlet. It's exhausting, causing some people to shut down so as not to be consumed by grief.

Occasionally it is good, necessary, and emotionally healthy to shut the door on the pain you are experiencing so that you can get through a task. If we keep the door open all the time, it can incapacitate us. The problem is sometimes people shut the door and realize life is easier without the messiness of emotions and decide to lock the door for the duration of the transition and possibly for good. Part of finishing well is knowing when to open the door. Brené Brown says we can't numb the bad without numbing the good.[38] The ability to allow others to finish well will be influenced by your emotional capacity to experience and process all of the pain you will be exposed to. There will be times to close the door to the pain as well as times to open it and experience the pain; the more you are able to do both, the more you will be able to be present with others during the transition.

Not all transitions are equal

My parents' garden was an especially fertile environment for mint, resulting in the extrication being more of a challenge than anticipated. However, mint was not the only plant in that garden. It also housed a bleeding-heart plant. While I haven't actually tried to remove it yet, I think it would be relatively easy to remove because there is just one plant. (But I could be dead wrong, seeing as my track record on plant knowledge is less than impressive.) I might need to dig a hole to get out all of the roots, but I'm fairly certain I wouldn't be going from one end of the garden to the other to remove the bleeding-heart. (I'm trying very hard not to use the word "weeding" even though that is what it felt like as the task went on!) Removing mint and removing the bleeding-heart would be very different tasks in the amount of time, energy, emotion invested, and scope of each project. Not all plant removal turns into a weeding nightmare. Likewise, not all transitions are equal.

While you can learn from other transitions you have gone through and from others who have gone through transitions, no one has gone through the exact transition you face. The American Automotive Association (AAA) provides wonderful traveling resources complete with maps, housing information, and traveling tidbits. But they cannot give you specifics about your trip before it happens because each trip is unique based on a variety of factors such as weather, traveling companions, and budget and time constraints. What it means to allow others to finish well with you will vary based on the type of transition you are going through. It's helpful to think through other transitions you've had and the people who needed to finish well. As you look back, how did you do? Were you able to allow them to finish well or is that an area you'd like to approach differently this time? How will this transition be different?

Let's look at who may need to finish well and what it might look like. For the sake of clarity, first we'll look at three scenarios and who might need to finish well outside of you and your family and then we'll explore ways they can finish well.

- Moving to another city within your organization (being relocated, going on home assignment, or choosing to move)
- Resigning from a job
- Moving countries, either transitioning onto or off the field

Moving to another city within your organization

We live in transient times, and if you stay with an organization long enough, the needs of your original call, your organization, or your family will likely lead to a move. While it can be a big fat hassle to move, most of us do not live in the same neighborhood we grew up in, which proves that the hassle doesn't stop us from moving. If you are moving out of the area, you will have a much larger cross-section of people for whom you will need to create "finishing well" space. Additionally, if you are married or have children, there will need to be combinations of individuals who will finish well with you: couples, kids, and families as well. Think through neighbors, co-workers, church groups, clubs, sports, friends, classmates, and family members who might want time with you. You might have a rather long list! As a family, sit down and rank people or groups as to how important they are to you. Remember, not all relationships are equal, and if you're not careful, you might end up spending time with people you don't really want to out of obligation instead of with those who are really important to you. These are not easy decisions to make in the crux of your transition, so think through them at more neutral times.

Resigning from a job

If you are moving from one job to another, the primary group you will need to allow to finish well is your co-workers from your old job. Again, be sensitive that you are moving toward something new and leaving them with a bit of a hole. While it might be more comfortable for you to leave with as little fuss as possible for a variety of reasons (e.g., maybe they haven't hired a replacement for you yet or you're leaving them mid-project and they are going to have to take over for you), remember it is not just about you. Part of you finishing well means you allow others to finish well with you.

Moving countries, either transitioning onto or off the field

This scenario will come with the greatest amount of relational energy because most everyone in your current life will not be in your future destination. Jobs, housing, and relationships will experience seismic changes. I moved to the field in August, and I remember when it hit me in November that there was not one person in my daily life who had known me more than four months. While exhilarating to start a new adventure, the overlap between my old self and my current self only occurred when my parents called. To this day, my teammate Erin refers to my friend Amy as "Kidney Amy" because Amy had recently donated a kidney to her brother before Erin and I met. Erin needed to learn the names and relationships of all my friends and family (and I needed to learn hers). To go from being fully known to having dear friends known as "Kidney Amy" or "the sister in Denver" or "the sister in Minneapolis" shows the potential extent of the transition and how important it is to allow others to finish well.

The above lists are not exhaustive in the people you may need to consider, but hopefully they have sparked your brainstorming about people whom you need to finish well.

It's all good and well to talk about this, but now that we've identified them, what does it mean practically to allow others to finish well? I chose the word *allow* over *help* because a significant part of it involves your attitude. *Help* focuses too much on what you do, whereas *allow* also creates space for your inner thoughts and attitudes to be gracious.

In essence, the goal is to provide others the opportunity to acknowledge that a phase of life is coming to an end. The way they choose to do that may or may not be a way you would choose. Ironically, for some it might mean they will want to just walk out the door and not do anything (for the very same reason you might want to: saying goodbye hurts and a natural response to pain is to turn away from it instead of leaning into it). While this isn't a good option for anyone, they might not know a better way, and you will need to accept it as what they are able to offer.

However, for those who are able, this opportunity is a gift that gives both ways: as someone finishes well with you, you can finish well with them. We've already looked at tasks (e.g., handling legal issues and possessions); this section will take a deeper look at what it means relationally. Simply, finishing well for relationships involves three parts: marking, blessing, and release. My explanation of the "how" of each of these is influenced by the concept of love languages in Dr. Gary Chapman's book *The Five Love Languages*.[39] Dr. Chapman explains that while we all give and receive love, we don't necessarily do it in the same way and will have preferences. The five languages include

It's Not Just About You

words of affirmation, quality time, receiving gifts, acts of service, and physical touch. The variety among the love languages and your understanding of them will lead to freedom and creativity as you mark, bless, and release people.

Marking

A passage in the Bible that speaks to marking involves the Israelites preparing to enter the Promised Land after forty long years of wandering in the wilderness. Talk about something finally coming to an end and a new chapter starting! When the people finished crossing the Jordan River, twelve men were sent back into the middle of the dried river bed to each get—or heft, as *The Message* puts it—a stone representing the twelve tribes of Israel. The stones were to serve as "a sign among you" so in the future children would ask what the stones mean. In answering this question the people would remember their history. It wasn't enough to promise themselves that they would remember; there needed to be some way to mark the significant event.

Part of finishing well relationally is to find ways to mark that *this* relationship, *this* person has mattered to you. "Stones of remembrance" can be done individually, in small groups, or in larger gatherings—it can be as simple as a goodbye card or a shared meal or as elaborate as a themed party. See the lists below for marking ideas for each of the five love languages.

Words of affirmation
- Write a handwritten card with a personal message.
- Schedule a time to tell them in person. Think through how this person mattered to you and made a difference in your life. Then share what you've learned from them and how you will incorporate it into your life.
- Put together a scrapbook with messages from everyone in your group (e.g., co-workers, family members, or Bible study group).

Looming Transitions

Quality time

- If possible, go on a trip or a weekend retreat or getaway together.
- If you have a routine, such as weekly lunches, regular walks, or a TV show you watch together, don't let it get squeezed out in the busyness of the last weeks or months. Continue the ritual as a gift to your friend or family member.

Giving and receiving gifts

- It's not about the size or cost of the gift but the thought or meaning that goes into it.
- Make a gift related to that person. For example, if they love movies, compile a list of movies that remind you of them. A friend, who was moving to a new city, wrote to all of her friends and asked for titles of their favorite books, which she compiled as lists to give to each friend. In another situation, I found an elastic hairband with a slot for a photo (I know, the things people come up with). Well, I got it for my friend Lisa who was moving and put a picture of me in it from a birthday party she had thrown for me. We enjoyed going to the gym together, and I told her to wear it to the gym in her new city. Whether she ever wore it or not, that silly hairband didn't cost much, but it was a way to mark our relationship and let her know she mattered.

Acts of service

- A person with this type of love language will mark the importance of your relationship by finding ways to serve you. It could be through helping with packing, cooking meals, providing childcare, or running errands for you.
- If your friends or family have this love language, look for specific ways they can serve you. The tricky reality may be that if this isn't your love language and you view acts of service as a burden, you may tend to avoid asking your friends for favors because you wouldn't want to burden them—or them to burden you if you were in their shoes.

It's Not Just About You

But you need to understand, for some it isn't a burden; rather, it is a way they are able to place a stone of remembrance and show you how much you matter to them.

Physical touch

- All of the love languages can feel a bit artificial or shallow if they're not your primary love language, but when it comes to physical touch, it can be downright awkward if that is not your love language. While you certainly aren't obliged to be hugged or touched by people who don't know you well, there will be some who will want to pat you on the arm or hug you more than normal. Touch can be a very powerful thing when it comes to marking something important, as is seen by the tradition of laying hands on someone during prayer.
- In the thick of your transition, you may need to accept that you might be touched more than you would prefer (or, if touch is your love language, not as much as you might like as some start to pull away). Remind yourself it's not just about you and people may need either to reach out or to pull away. Give them the gift of receiving whatever it is they offer.

Combination of love languages

Life is not always neatly divided into these five areas of expressing love. Sometimes the way you mark a relationship with a loved one will involve multiple love languages. When I graduated from seminary, there were four of us who had helped carry each other through, and I wanted to find a way to mark and honor our experiences. I bought each a copy of *Through Painted Deserts* by Donald Miller[40] and wrote the following in the front (combining gifts and words of affirmation):

> Dearest Karen, Katie, and Matt,
> I know we are familiar with the biblical tradition of "stones of remembrance" to mark a significant event in which the Lord has been faithful. In wanting to mark

getting a counseling degree and indicate the significant role you have played, I decided to give you each *Through Painted Deserts.* I chose this book because it chronicles a road trip from Austin to the NW taken by the author and a man he didn't really know at the start of the journey. It was during the journey they became friends. Sound familiar? I hardly knew two years ago where this would take me, but here we are and I am simply not the same as I was at the start of the journey.

There are a few quotations that in particular made me think of our journey:
- See "page x" in the introduction that talks about keeping our souls fertile. This is my prayer for you as life continues to unfold.
- "It turns out the droplet of our knowledge is a bit lost in the ocean of our unknowing" (p. 26). Isn't that great!!! That is how I feel here at the end . . . we have worked hard and studied a ton, but isn't that ocean huge?
- "It is difficult to recall, much less recapture, the excitement of an adventure's beginning when you find yourself in the boring middle of it" (p. 89). Doesn't this vividly capture hours spent in the library?

Thank you, my friends, for the love and acceptance you have shown me. I love you each and am grateful to have traveled with you.

Love, Amy

Blessing (or Curse)

James 3:10 reminds us that out of the same mouth come blessings as well as curses. While you might be sad (or friends or family may be sad) about what is coming to an end, your transition is a powerful time to offer a blessing for the next phase of life. Unfortunately it's also a time when out of your sadness you may curse via being passive-aggressive or manipulative. Part of finishing well is to bless instead of curse. The act of blessing is powerful because it shows that you want the very best for the person you are blessing (whether you are the one moving on or staying). Most importantly, because they have blessed your life, you want others to be blessed as well.

Blessing can be done either individually or corporately and in many forms. It most often is in the form of words, but it can also involve a gift and physical touch. They can involve saying a personalized blessing or using a scripture such as Numbers 6:24-26 (NIV):

> *"The LORD bless you*
> *and keep you;*
> *the LORD make his face shine upon you*
> *and be gracious to you;*
> *the LORD turn his face toward you*
> *and give you peace."*

Or there are a number of Irish blessings such as this one:[41]

> *May the road rise up to meet you.*
> *May the wind always be at your back.*
> *May the sun shine warm upon your face,*
> *and rains fall soft upon your fields.*
> *And until we meet again,*
> *May God hold you in the palm of His hand.*

Don't rush this phase. I know that it can feel a bit awkward to bless someone, but it is worth it to push through the discomfort. Look into their eyes and be present in the moment. John Ortberg has a powerful chapter in his book *Soul Keeping*[42] on how to extend blessings to others if you'd like more information.

Release

After marking the relationship and blessing the person, the final aspect is the release. This part of the process is internal and will differ depending on the nature of each relationship. It is impossible for your relationships to go on as they have with no change. The people you are releasing will no longer be in your house twenty-four seven; you will no longer be working with those people every day; your spouse will now be home every day instead of in the office (Lord have mercy on you both!). Change is a comin', so to create space for your new reality, you need to release certain individuals to go forward even if it is somewhere you do not want them to go. Raising grandchildren in another country from their grandparents? No, thank you. Returning to your home country for a dream job or additional training? Well, maybe mostly yes!

The release involves being able to let change come even if it means you won't be as close emotionally or physically. It is brave to say, "Come what may, I will not play guilt trips or manipulate you. I will celebrate what I can about this change and not hold on to the past." Some relationships will deepen in and through the transition and others will die. All will have parts that are messy.

We see this with Jesus and at least two of his disciples. At what has come to be known as the Last Supper, it was obvious that change was coming, although the disciples didn't fully know what was next. Jesus had to release each disciple regardless of how each man would treat him or how their relationship would change. Painfully, in this process of release, Judas betrayed him and Peter denied him. I don't want to psychoanalyze and read into the text more than is there or try to guess at their motives other than to say that change can feel threatening and doesn't always bring out our best, to say the very least. Both men regretted their actions, with Peter weeping bitterly and Judas being seized by remorse. Ultimately Peter's relationship with Jesus was restored and experienced a new level of depth. However, Judas took his own life; not every release will end so tragically, of course. These examples showcase that a true release comes with no guarantees other than the fact that the relationship will not continue as it has in the past.

It's Not Just About You

The two-sidedness of this coin is that the release opens the door for a different kind of relationship with the potential for richness that can only be reached through this metamorphosis. Or it may wither a bit and lose some of the vigor of its blossom. And like the song "Delta Dawn," it may grow to be a "faded rose from days gone by." That does not diminish its significance in your story. Since our seminary graduation, I have only seen Matt once; last I heard he's somewhere in California. Karen's gotten married. I stay in contact with Katie, although it's not the same as those long days spent in the library. We have moved from fellow soldiers in our pursuit of an education to veterans of those hallowed halls.

Mark the relationship.
Bless those in it.
Release them to a different status.

Feeling limp

Here's the thing, though, about letting others finish well: it's exhausting. Although many of your friends and family will be part of just one or two goodbye events, you have to attend them all. It's natural to detach and want to simply have this phase over. While you don't need to be a martyr and there *will* be times when it is okay to say no, say yes to what you can and give others the gift of finishing well. This will be easier for some than for others, but it's important for all.

Chapter 9

Work Out Your Grief

Farming looks mighty easy when your plow is a pencil and you're a thousand miles from the corn field.
—Dwight D. Eisenhower

Love anything and your heart will certainly be wrung and possibly broken.
—C. S. Lewis

There are two kinds of people in the world: those who believe infomercials and those who don't. I come from a mixed family with half in one camp and half in the other. Those of us in the "we never met an infomercial when we were channel surfing that we didn't want to watch for at least five minutes" camp would probably admit in our more rational moments that they promise more than can be delivered. Wouldn't it be wonderful if for only $29.99 (plus shipping and handling) and just thirty minutes a day you could "have the body you've always wanted"? Sign me up for that! The problem is it's simply not true. There have been tests done—at least I saw a report on the *Today* show—on many of the products offered on infomercials, and most of them do not deliver. But infomercials continue to be a thriving business. Why? Because as much as we know we can't have it, we want something for nothing. We want to live in a world where life is easy and where the laws of reaping and sowing don't apply. At least not to us.

But that's not the world we live in.

Work Out Your Grief

You cannot come to the end of a life chapter without it, well, ending. And often not in one big, final ending but in a thousand mini-deaths. While some deaths are a relief (that pesky co-worker, the traffic in your city, shoveling snow), plenty others about your current life will be missed. Infomercial land would promise you that for only three easy payments you can bypass the painful parts of a change that is akin to something dying, but they are lying. Death is now a part of your story. But as scripture points out, "We do not mourn as those who have no hope."[43] It doesn't say that that we do not mourn. We mourn. But with hope. We are called back to the paradox of the messy middle. On the one side is open and raw mourning and on the other, beautiful, awe-inspiring, hope. And there you are with part in each camp.

C.S. Lewis got it right when he wrote, "Love anything and your heart will certainly be wrung and possibly broken." Whether you are a pre- or a post-griever, your heart is going to be wrung, and maybe broken, as this phase of life comes to an end. Even if wonderfulness awaits you on the other side, in the form of a newfound freedom or challenge or relationship, the positive does not negate the elements of grief. We humans are complex and can feel multiple things at once. As painful as it will be, it's important to turn toward the pain of grieving instead of turning away.

Unfortunately, this is not the message we are fed by our society. Instead we are encouraged to avoid pain—any form—at all cost. Ways to self-medicate and escape pain come in forms both sanctioned and frowned upon by society at large. You can avoid pain with TV, alcohol, sleep, work, pornography, thrill-seeking, drugs, or just keeping yourself too busy. I am not advocating pain for the sake of pain; having had several minor surgeries without anesthesia and been told just to "bear it" cured me of romanticizing pain! But when something is painful and we don't acknowledge it, we end up leaking all over. Leaking can show up as detachment, anger, or disillusionment, in addition to the ways we self-medicate.

Looming Transitions

Is detachment a viable option at times so that you can get through a certain time period, event, or conversation? Of course. But notice how often a behavior occurs, such as having a shorter temper than normal or telling a loved one you don't want to talk about *it* and you have quite a long list of *its*. Is that behavior becoming your go-to coping mechanism? One way to determine if a behavior is not a healthy way of coping is to ask yourself the question of whether it is serving you or you are serving it as your master. If it is serving you, you move toward God, people, relationships, and meaningful interactions. Coping mechanisms that have become like masters, on the other hand, will create space and distance, moving you further away from people, feelings, and interactions that bring meaningful connection.

When I was a child, we had a compost pile in our backyard. The compost pile was a necessary step for transforming unneeded food (like carrot tops, egg shells, and apple cores) into fertilizer. While we could take the banana peels and coffee grounds and toss them into our garden, they were more effective as fertilizer if allowed the time to decompose and mix together. Part of keeping your soul fertile is allowing this leg of your life journey the space and time to turn into fertilizer for the next phase of life that will be planted in you—in your talents, your relationships, your soul. The compost pile of our souls is grief.

Compost piles are often at the back of a garden or maybe off in a non-descript container. It's understandable that given their lack of beauty and unpleasant odor they are not a prominent feature of most gardens. But it's not only their appearance that relegates them to the corner; it's also because they take time and need a space set apart to ferment. There is an element of time with compost that can't be pushed too much. The process can be sped up by adding moisture, stirring the compost pile, and exposing it to heat and light. These are catalysts that can speed up the process to a certain point, but they can't replace the process itself. The elements must be allowed to convert from one state into another. Grief is similar. There are things that can be done to share it and soften it, but a point comes when you will still a viable option at times so that you can get ___ time period, event, or conversation? Of course, ___ often a behavior occurs, such as having a shorter ___ normal or telling a loved one you don't want to ___ and you have quite a long list of *its*. Is that behavior beco__ your go-to coping mechanism? One way to determine if a behavior is not a healthy way of coping is to ask yourself the question of whether it is serving you or you are serving it as your master. If it is serving you, you move toward God, people, relationships, and meaningful interactions. Coping mechanisms that have become like masters, on the other hand, will create space and distance, moving you further away from people, feelings, and interactions that bring meaningful connection.

When I was a child, we had a compost pile in our backyard. The compost pile was a necessary step for transforming unneeded food (like carrot tops, egg shells, and apple cores) into fertilizer. While we could take the banana peels and coffee grounds and toss them into our garden, they were more effective as fertilizer if allowed the time to decompose and mix together. Part of keeping your soul fertile is allowing this leg of your life journey the space and time to turn into fertilizer for the next phase of life that will be planted in you—in your talents, your relationships, your soul. The compost pile of our souls is grief.

Compost piles are often at the back of a garden or maybe off in a non-descript container. It's understandable that given their lack of beauty and unpleasant odor they are not a prominent feature of most gardens. But it's not only their appearance that relegates them to the corner; it's also because they take time and need a space set apart to ferment. There is an element of time with compost that can't be pushed too much. The process can be sped up by adding moisture, stirring the compost pile, and exposing it to heat and light. These are catalysts that can speed up the process to a certain point, but they can't replace the process itself. The elements must be allowed to convert from one state into another. Grief is similar. There are things that can be done to share it and soften it, but a point comes when you will still

Work Out Your Grief

need to turn, face your grief, and walk into it.

In the book of Philippians, Paul uses the phrase "to work out our salvation."[44] The Greek word for "work out"—κατεργάζομαι (katergazomai)—means to achieve, accomplish, bring about, produce, or create.[45] Look at those verbs! They are active. Achieve. Accomplish. Bring about. Produce. Create. They do not involve sitting, waiting, ignoring, or passing the time. No, they are out-there verbs. The grief involving a season of life ending is different from the unexpected loss of a family member or friend, which knocks you over. The type we're dealing with here is less sudden; knowing that the loss is coming allows you the luxury of "working out your grief" even before the loss occurs. Turning and facing your grief about a season's ending involves more than standing and letting grief wash over you in waves. There are things you can do to manage your grief in order to finish a transition well.

During my twenty-year service, I spent three years on a study leave in the U.S. earning an MA. When I was preparing to return to China after living with my parents, I found many people didn't know how to respond when I would share the loss I was experiencing. I had returned to the U.S. for three years to attend graduate school. Returning to China was not a surprise, and actually I was right on schedule to do so. But there were daily rhythms I was going to miss and activities *I* wanted to participate in. When I told people I was sad—and even felt a bit guilty I wouldn't be able to help my parents shovel snow the next winter—without missing a beat almost everyone responded the same way: "Oh, don't worry, God will provide for your parents." I wanted to spit back: *I do not doubt that! I know God will provide; what you are missing is that I want it to be ME he uses to provide for them.* At times I'd provide a more socially appropriate response (sans spittle and venom); other times I'd just let it go with a sad sigh on the inside, feeling that instead of "getting it" and moving toward me in my grief, they missed what I was saying and moved away from me.

Of course, not everyone is going to be a safe person who gets your grief. But part of the conundrum is not all situations involving grief look like something to be grieved. If people stopped and looked and thought before they spoke, they might see below the surface to what it is you need to grieve. They would be able to hold two truths at once. Job well done on raising a child *and* what a hole your family will have as you transition them off the field and to college. How exciting to be moving to another country in response to God's call *and* what a bummer you won't be able to watch football games with your friends in person. They are both true. One doesn't negate the other. In a mysterious way they complete each other like two distinct sides of a coin.

Unfortunately, too many people are uncomfortable with pain, and to alleviate it they swoop in with platitudes. It might be aiming too high, but I hope a small revolution of grieving well with one another can start with you and the example you set during your transition.

How do you go about grieving parts of life that are slow in coming? Or are not clearly marked? Or come with many small losses? Or, more confusingly, are marked with celebration as well? Thankfully, there are three easy steps to grieving. Well, that would be true if we lived in Infomercial-ville, which we don't. Instead we live in a muddled world that is often uncomfortable with grief. We are not left helpless without a game plan, however. Turns out, three steps exist, and you can do them all. Sometimes it will be easy to follow them; other times not at all. That's the plain and messy truth. They are:

Tune in.
Name it.
Grieve it.

Tune in

Part of finishing well is grieving well. The challenge comes in the number of small deaths you will encounter and their obviousness. Losses are going to be subtly woven throughout daily life, and the way you experience and process them will be influ-

Work Out Your Grief

enced by your personality, family of origin, and culture. Because of this the first step is to tune in. Part of tuning in means you give yourself the space to sort through your stress and grief on a regular basis. This could be semantic hair-splitting given that stress and grief can be intermingled. Look beneath the surface and try to identify whether the root is "merely" stress or if there is an aspect of loss.

As with stress, grief comes with physical and emotional reactions. Let's be honest, it is exhausting to grieve. Some of the physical symptoms include fatigue, lethargy, changes in sleep and dreaming patterns, changes in appetite resulting in weight loss or gain, nervousness, racing heart rate, and unexplained aches and pains. This is not an exhaustive list, but you get the idea that the impact of grief can manifest negatively in our bodies. Grief can also cause emotional reactions, such as anger, sadness, numbness, feelings of guilt, feelings of blame, or feelings of resentment. And while there is no "right" way to grieve, it does help to be aware of the process of grief.

For example, going grocery shopping has the potential to be stressful in and of itself (or relaxing, depending on your personality, financial resources, and time frame). If your time is limited because there are many things on your to-do list related to the upcoming transition, your stress might be merely stress without grief. The word "merely" is not meant to minimize but to isolate the source. But if while shopping you find yourself snappish, aloof, or weepy, stop and tune in. Maybe what's behind your reaction is the stress of knowing the city you're moving to doesn't have the store or the brands you like. Or maybe the thought of having to learn where everything is in a new store just seems overwhelming and you're limp at the thought of yet another loss. This is more rooted in grief. While grief and stress are relatives, they are not identical twins.

Though times of transition are known for all that needs to be done, tuning in will also involve slowing down and maybe even stopping every now and then. In *The Poisonwood Bible* by Barbara Kingsolver, Orleanna, the mother of four daughters, offers this insight after the death of her youngest, Ruth May: "As long as I kept moving, my grief streamed out behind me like a swimmer's long hair in water. I knew the weight was there but it didn't touch me. Only when I stopped did the slick, dark stuff of it come floating in around my face, catching my arms and throat till I began to drown. So I just didn't stop."[46]

That right there is worth pausing over. *Only when I stopped did it catch up with me. So I just didn't stop.* We are a culture of non-stoppers. Just keep moving, no matter what. Transitions present the perfect time to run from grief by simply keeping moving. Your life will demand so much motion. But your soul demands stillness. And how scary stillness can be because then grief can catch you. Motion isn't the problem. Movement is good. The problem comes when we self-medicate by filling our lives to the brim and don't allow grief to catch up with us, so we can see it and deal with it.. I asked a friend to list all of her losses and nearly forty filled the page front and back; she could have gone on, but there was no paper left. She said it was depressing at first, but by the end she felt validated in her sadness and a bit lighter.

Tuning in isn't just contemplating your feelings; it's about sorting out pieces of your life and story so you can process your grief in a healthy way. Each of the multiple small deaths you will face will not come packaged the same way, so it is vital that you tune in.

Name it

Want to know one of the scariest things we can do during the grief process? Name our grief. A father appears not to be supportive of his adult daughter moving overseas, when in fact he is grieving that she won't need him the way she has. A soccer buddy moves back home to go to grad school and the other athletic person on the team is annoyed that no one else in her city wants to play soccer; she's more than annoyed. A grandmother grieving she won't be able to help with childcare when her grandkids live abroad. A teammate grieving the change in holiday traditions when the only person who makes potatoes the ways he likes is moving to another assignment. There is nothing wrong in any of the above scenarios, but the element of grief is not always named. Dad's just being difficult, the athlete temperamental, the grandmother selfish, and the teammate too sentimental. While those all may be true, there are aspects to be grieved in each of the scenarios.

Naming something is more powerful than describing it. Consider the following interaction:

Person A: *Do you see the tall man wearing the blue shirt and pointing with his left hand?*

Person B: *Do you mean Tom?*

Person A: *Um, yeah.*

Just as the shortest way between two points is a straight line, the simplest way to get to the essence of grief is to name it. *Do you see that person being snappish, standoffish, tired, and eating more than normal?* Do you mean the one grieving? *Um, yeah.* Once you have tuned into your grief, label it as such. It's fine to describe it as well, but describing sometimes falls short of the raw honesty of naming grief for what it is. Look at the following two sentences:

I haven't been sleeping well.

I haven't been sleeping well because I'm grieving.

The difference is deeper than the three words tagged on. Although both are true, the second statement opens up a truth because it goes to a deeper level. Not everything needs to be named publicly. When I say the second step is to name your grief, the primary person you need to name it to is yourself.

I was a hot mess my last year in China. When I walked home from the gym, I cried. Almost every time. I did my best to pretend nothing was happening around my eyes because crying is so not cool in a country that's all about maintaining "face" in public. I didn't tend to cry in other beloved places, so in overanalyzing this odd pattern, I came to this insight: The gym was the purest expression of what I would miss. I'm one of the best (although not most lovely or graceful) versions of myself when I'm exercising. The reasons I was leaving the field were complicated and parts were not appropriate for public knowledge. The sense of loss was profound, and I didn't appreciate being in a clichéd mid-life crisis. Wasn't serving God supposed to make one immune to such struggles? But that gym held memories of normal life, funny stories, and friendships. It had nothing to do with the complications of the move, and when I walked home, the sweetness and purity of what the gym represented flooded me with emotion.

Once you know what's happening beyond the surface and have been able to name it, you can decide who needs to know. For some that will be a fairly long list; for others it will be a short list. The length of the list is probably tied more to personality and age than to emotional health. The point is not how long your list is. After you have identified you are grieving, can you take the brave and sometimes scary step in naming it to those on your list? Being able to recognize you are grieving and label it as such, including sharing your revelation with a carefully selected group of close friends and family, is a significant part of finishing well.

Grieve it

And now we get to the action part of grieving. Because you'll die a thousand mini-deaths, there will not be one way to grieve. Instead in the messy middle there are as many ways to grieve as there are things to be grieved! Missing Trader Joe's is not the same as missing a dear friend after moving to another city. Are they both losses? Yes, and sometimes in the messiness of grieving, the two might get mixed up. Suddenly you care so much about Trader Joe's (or your favorite market), you can't imagine shopping anywhere else for groceries while your friendship, for some reason, doesn't feel like a big loss. Even with tuning in and naming grief, we can still get some parts confused as we try to avoid pain. The act of grieving a long goodbye can range from simply tuning in and naming it to bigger forms of action—the working out of your grief that I mentioned earlier. Here are some ideas:

Often tears are involved. Crying is natural when someone is grieving, and it actually helps to process the emotions. The amount of crying will vary person to person and should not be seen as a reflection of how much a person, place, or routine will be missed. Every person, family, and culture has different rules and values about crying. When is it okay to cry? Who can cry? How long is it appropriate to cry? Is crying a sign of strength or weakness? Take a moment to think through your family's and culture's norms and taboos when it comes to crying. How would you summarize them in one or two sentences? How are they different from those of other families you know? You are the expert on yourself, so you will know best whether you will need to cry or not.

Think through the values you have about crying and, if you're a parent, the beliefs and values you have about your kids crying. Reflecting back on other times you have mourned, are there things you would like to change about the way you mourn? Remember that emotional reactions are not always timely when it comes to major changes, and if you find yourself crying more than normal during your transition, that's perfectly normal. It's also to be expected if there are times when the waves of emotion are too much and you shut them down for the time being. The challenge is that transitions are busy, and finding the time to feel difficult emotions without ignoring and postponing them too much can be tricky. Tricky but not impossible. The more you're able to keep a short account of things for later, the better.

The timing of crying may be out of your control, but thankfully not all parts of grieving have to be. This might sound a bit morbid, but have a funeral or two. What is the point of a funeral? It is a way to mark the end of a life and publicly proclaim that the person who died mattered and will be missed. Funerals also allow for corporate commemorating. As you work out your grief, the "funerals" you hold mark the end you are experiencing. It might be a final meal at a favorite restaurant, a card, a gift, or a goodbye party. More than "being the right thing to do," these practices help to work out grief. In the process of throwing a goodbye party, for example, each act of preparation is a way to bring physicality to the nebulous sense of loss. Making lists, going shopping, or setting up for the event involves your body and not just emotions in this phase.

The idea of working out your grief is broader than group activities such as parties or meals. Remember my friend who gave me a list of book recommendations as she prepared to move back to the U.S.? Her gift illustrates the importance of the process in dealing with grief: the task of choosing something important to me, contacting her friends, reading their ideas, compiling the list, and having it laminated were all ways for her to grieve.

Maybe you're wondering, what if I didn't like the recommended books? And here we come to another important point in the grieving process: be clear in your mind whom this gesture is for. Did it matter if I liked the books? On one level, of course my friend wanted to give me something that I would enjoy and appreciate. In this case, I did, obviously as I remember it all these years later and have mentioned it twice. But liking is not the point.

Funerals, similarly, are not for the dead. The deceased is not aware of the event, the people attending, the music, the tears, the cards, or the flowers. Ultimately memorial services and funerals are for those who are grieving. Likewise, a present has more to offer the giver than the recipient, regardless of how much you know that they will "just love it."

It is key we get this one right. When my friend compiled the book list for me, yes, she chose something important to me (books) and I was touched by the effort she went to, but ultimately the very act of compiling it was for her to mourn. With each gesture you plan, are you doing it because it is helping you to work out your grief, because it is the socially expected thing to do, or because you are hoping for a reaction from others? It is essential that as much as possible, we search out our motives, not to change them but to be aware of them so that others' opinions and reactions are not the focus.

This point hit home for me when I was preparing to return to China after living in the U.S. for three years. My sister and her family lived nearby, and the thought of leaving young nieces after getting to be a part of their daily lives felt akin to having a lung ripped out of my chest. As I wondered what I could give them as a sign of how important and fun those three years had been, I needed a project with stages and steps to help me start to walk toward the goodbye. The challenge is I am not artistic, creative, or patient with things that require a high degree of detail; I also wanted a project I would actually be able to complete. At Michael's craft store I hit on the idea of decorating a pillowcase for each girl. Loaded up with an array of colors and stencils, I started personalizing pillowcases with each of my nieces' names written in a different style, decorating them with dainty bugs and flowers. I worked on these gifts for over a week. I would add a flower to Emily's, then a bug to Katy's or Anna's pillowcase as Emily's was drying. As I worked, I let the tears come and go as I thought of how much I would miss each one, how I had enjoyed watching Katy learn to walk. I considered the parallels between preschool and graduate school the year Emily and I respectively "started school." I mourned that Anna was only two and wouldn't remember that I had once been a part of her daily life. I painted and grieved. I painted and thought of each girl. This was years ago and even now the tears well as I recall this project.

When the pillowcases were done, I wrapped them and took them over to my sister's house on the last Saturday before I left. The girls opened their gifts, and that was the last I saw or heard of those pillowcases. And while I was a bit surprised by their lackluster reaction—just being honest, because I thought they were pretty cool—their reactions helped me to clarify my motives behind the project. Maybe their reactions lacked enthusiasm because of their age, or maybe they were grieving too. But ultimately it wasn't just a gift for them. I started the project as a way to mourn, a way to bring a physical component to my grief. I needed a way to mark I was not going to be the same "Aunt Amy" I had been for three years. I had come to know them as individuals, and the void of not having them in my daily life would be both deep and wide.

When you look for ways to physically work out or mark your grief, check your motives. It's easier to start off on one path and along the way get distracted and end up somewhere you hadn't planned to go. If you start a project to help you work out your grief, stop every now and then to double-check you are still on the path and haven't taken a detour that leads you to "Others-will-be-amazed-by-this-ville!" or "I-started-off-doing-this-for-me-but-now-I'm-really-doing-this-for-you-land." Some ideas will end up being both: a way for you to work out your grief and a touching present or experience for the sake of another. Getting tripped up by unknown expectations will still happen even if you are checking your motives. But hopefully you'll recognize them quickly, and they won't overrun your grief process and make the focus on the gesture.

Working out your grief is a process that won't end just because you had a plan and found ways to work it out ahead of time. You will continue to grieve. Even now I envision myself in Michael's scouring the shelves for supplies and paint, and tears well in my eyes as I type. If I could go back in time and put my arm around that Amy who traced bugs on pillowcases, I would tell her it won't always hurt as much as it does now, but there will always be an ache. Working out your grief does not mean you can or even should avoid the pain; instead it means you face the pain and walk into it. You feel it. And it is real. And it comes in waves. And some days are easier than others. But you also cling to the truth that we do not mourn as those who have no hope.

Going on a bear hunt

Of all the areas we've looked at in these chapters, grieving is the one most likely to continue long after you have finished well

Work Out Your Grief

in your transition. Remember the children's chant about going on a bear hunt? I hear the chant "I'm not afraid!" echoing in my head. On your proverbial bear hunt, when you come up to woods or a hill or some tall grasses, what are you going to do? Can't go around it, can't go over it, and can't go under it: got to go through it. Don't buy the lie that sorrow can be avoided by going around, over, or under it. It can't. Sorrow that is avoided will hunt *you* down and show up as shut-down emotions, distance in relationships, confusing reactions to events, some form of physical manifestations, even in your interactions with God. We know that ulcers are not always caused by an inability to digest food. Some are brought on by an inability to digest grief. Headaches sometimes are manifestations of heartaches. Anxiety and stress are ways of saying, "It hurts so much to think of life without you that I can't bear it."

In the bear hunt song, there is only one way to catch the bear: to go through the woods. On your quest to finish well, you will encounter people, places, and possessions you will grieve, and you will have a choice: are you going to try to go around your grief or through it? Either way, life will go on, but by tuning in to what's going on in you, naming it, and then grieving it, you allow this stage of your life to be mixed and churned together in such a way that it becomes fertilizer for your soul.

Chapter 10

Your Unique Path

Each soil has had its own history. Like a river, a mountain, a forest, or any natural thing, its present condition is due to the influences of many things and events of the past.
—Charles Kellogg

Jesus Christ is the same yesterday and today and forever.
—Hebrews 13:8

One of the truest statements I have ever read concerning the life of a cross-cultural worker came from an odd source, *The Pilgrim's Regress* by C. S. Lewis. He writes, "Be sure it is not for nothing that the Landlord has knit our hearts so closely to time and place—to one friend rather than another and one shire more than all the land."[47]

I first read this one summer when I was back in the U.S. visiting friends and family. My mom and sister were (and still are) in a book club. If you've lived overseas, love books, and have not been able to interact with others, you know the joy of discussing books with other book lovers. So even though July's book was *The Pilgrim's Regress* and I'm not normally drawn to allegory, I jumped at the chance to join in. It turned out to be the ideal book for me. That line explained succinctly what I felt deep in my soul but couldn't have articulated: I was knit to China. Yes, yes, I love the whole world. But for most of us, the whole world is too much to grasp and really love. It's true, I do love one shire more than all the land. If you're reading this book, I know you get

Your Unique Path

it. You've felt the stirring of one shire calling. For some you're moving from your home shire to a distant one and are beginning your journey. For others, the strings tying you to a distant shore have loosened and you're returning to your passport country (I hesitate to call it home) or on to another shore.

When I first went to the field, I was a doe-eyed twenty-four-year-old who still got spiral perms in my long hair. I still have the passport picture to prove it. In the midst of my time overseas, I transitioned back to the U.S. for three years of graduate study, after which I returned to the field for six more years. My most recent transition has been to relocate back to the U.S. I'm no longer doe-eyed, complete with transition lenses in my glasses; I've served in more than seven different roles on the field, some involving leadership, and I've lived a rich and significant life. It was disorienting and complex when the Landlord began to loosen the knitting from one shire and point me to another.

Will you ever live abroad again?

When people ask me this question, I don't know how to answer, and I'm asked it more often and in more contexts than I expected: by friends, casual acquaintances, people who've heard me speak or read my writing, and even strangers who find out I've relocated. Again and again, "Will you ever live abroad again?" Three years ago I thought I would retire in China with the organization I had been with for years. Having not called that one correctly, why would my answer now be any more accurate? I'm in my mid-forties, not my late sixties. I made a major transition only two years ago and then experienced the death of a parent a year into my relocation. Will I ever live abroad again? How do I know? Will the Denver Broncos win the Super Bowl? I don't know. But I hope so.

Often when people ask me the question, I sense that it's not just about me. Instead, there is a hint of fear and value attached to it. If our paths aren't the same, if I stay "gone" from abroad, this threatens some. Such pressure exists to be the same, to live parallel stories. If our lives are similar, neither of us have screwed up, we're both okay. So, as I heard this question, more than any other being asked over and over, I tuned in. You probably have an area in your life that is threatening too—although the people asking the question or making the comment may not realize they are revealing more about themselves than about you. *You have how many children?* With the number considered high or low. *You won't work late?* When you buck the norms of your job and leave to be home for dinner with the family. Same is comforting, different threatening.

The assumption is that if you're an "abroad" person, you need to stay an abroad person. By returning to the U.S., I've broken an unspoken rule and gone rogue. I didn't mean to. In my story, each major transition had similarities but also slight differences (we'll get to those soon). Every family, country, and organization has norms and rules that help to create stability and a sense of location within the story. Like me, you may feel you're going rogue too. Going off script in the best (or worst) sense, following in the footsteps of Abraham who was called to a distance shire when God said, "Go from your country, your people and your father's household to the land I will show you."[48]

In this chapter we are going to look at unique aspects of finishing well when it comes to preparing for five scenarios: (1) first time to the field, (2) first furlough or home assignment, (3) returning to the field after a furlough or home assignment, (4) subsequent furloughs and home assignments (including children starting college), (5) leaving the field for the foreseeable future.

Each scenario will also have five influential factors. Feel free to read through each scenario or just skip to the transition you are facing.

First time to the field

Before we go further, let me say, welcome and how exciting this phase is. Finally, right? Finally, after the stirring in your soul many moons ago, you're getting to go! As exciting as it is, though, I know whispers can creep in. Even though decades have passed and I am who I am today because of my time overseas, I sometimes wonder how things might have been different if I had not moved overseas. Before I went to the field, I was a junior high math teacher. I was low on the totem pole, and not only did I not have my own classroom, having to travel from room to room during other teachers' planning periods, but I also had to travel from school to school. After lunch duty at South Junior High, I hopped in my car and drove to West Junior High to spend the last two periods with seventh graders and algebraic principles. For early adulthood, I was living the dream.

But I heard the call to a different dream and was soon knee deep in never-ending to-do lists: securing a visa, packing up my life, getting legal affairs in order, and handling the ups and downs of raising support. My school district was opening a new school, and I was well into the process of preparing to go to the field. I was told that if I decided to stay and teach in the district, I would be assigned to the new school. To be a part of a staff that helped open a school and establish norms and rituals was—without exaggeration—a once-in-a-lifetime opportunity. Plus I would be in a brand-spanking-new facility and have my very own classroom. I would also be able to help students as they moved schools midway through junior high.

It gave me pause.

You will likely have your own pause. Part of finishing well is to count the cost and to acknowledge there is and will be a cost. It could be to your career; it could be to your earning potential; it could be to your time with family. My salary dropped 86 percent, and I was no longer an up-and-coming math teacher. But we know costs are not just financial, and part of the grieving process we've talked about involves them too. Your pause may be a chance to count the cost; it may also be God speaking to you. I know of a young woman who found out, just weeks before she left for the field, that her dad was diagnosed with an inoperable brain tumor and had one year to live. She decided the timing was God's pause for her not to go to the field and spend the year with her family. If the pause comes, don't beat yourself up. Know that it's part of the process.

Another part of moving overseas is making decisions on what to take with you in light of what you will or will not be able to buy in your new country. Finding ways to talk to others who live there and can fill you in on what is available in your new city will help to alleviate some of the ambiguity. This book is on finishing well, not focusing on the next phase; however, one tip to benefit the next phase is to begin now to factor in a margin of error. There are going to be things you bring with you, and you will later wonder why in heaven's name you hauled *this* or *that* around the world. There will be other times you will cry out in frustration saying, "If only I had known X, I would have brought Y!" Well, you didn't know X and you hauled *this* because you thought you would need or want it. Choose right now to make peace with the reality that you will not pack or prepare perfectly so that when those moments happen, you can chalk them up to your margin of error. This will help you to move on and not get stuck in regret or frustration.

A final warning for you first-timers: people will come out of the woodwork the last week before you leave. I don't know why this is, but having worked with well over a thousand people who have moved overseas, this is a recurring story. After months of knowing you are leaving and not getting around to seeing you, friends and family seem to sense a sudden urgency. I touched on this in Chapter 8, but I'll repeat it here: not all relationships are equal; you don't want to look back and realize you did not spend enough time with the people most important to you. Plan your final gatherings accordingly, and perhaps even have a trusted friend help you think through the requests and your responses.

Five questions for those preparing for the first time to the field:

1. Have you been able to visit your new country and taste what daily life will be like?

2. Do you have a clear sense of what you will be doing?

3. What is your stage in life: young single, young married couple without kids, young family, family with older kids who may not want to go, middle-aged single or married without kids, or older couple with grandkids. Also, do you have aging parents or grandparents?

4. What is the length of your initial commitment, and how long do you see yourself overseas?

5. What is the amount of family support emotionally and spiritually?

First furlough or home assignment

On the field I was also a teacher, and part of my contract included a ticket back home at the end of each academic year for a few weeks with my family—not a furlough in the traditional sense of an extended period of time back home after completing a four-year term. However, tell that to my heart and you might get a considerable amount of pushback. When our school officials dropped off the physical plane tickets, I was so excited I went straight to my teammate's classroom to share the news. As I sat in the back of her classroom waiting as time dragged until the ten-minute break in the two-hour class, she glanced at me and I held up a ticket; after making an excuse to get the students to occupy themselves, she came back to me and we silently squealed and marveled, through hushed whispers, that we would indeed be spending a few weeks home!

Our school used our apartments to house summer teachers, so even though we were returning for the fall semester, we had to pack everything up and store it in our wardrobes. As annoying as this was, it was more annoying at the end of each summer to unpack my worldly possessions from a summer boxed up in a humid and moldy environment. This was my story for the next five years. Well, there was the one summer when our apartments were renovated and we returned to find most boxes opened by curious migrant workers. I get it, I'm curious about their lives too. But the maddening part was that they had opened perishable items, like Jello, and left us torn bags that were now ruined because the humid air turned them into inedible bricks. Time away can be a mixed blessing, can't it?

Chances are your story won't have torn Jello packets in it, but I bet it will come with pockets of bubbling excitement and eagerly anticipated food and folks.

Five questions for those preparing for their first furlough or home assignment:

1. How long was your term of service?

2. How long will you be in your passport country?

3. Do you have looming needs in your marriage, parenting, or personal life?

4. Overall, was this first term positive or negative?

5. Regarding your setup while on furlough, do you have housing? A vehicle? How many locations do you need to visit? Will you need to raise additional funds for your next term?

Returning to the field after a furlough or home assignment

It was November, and I was returning to the field the following summer. I was talking with Charlie, my supervisor when I was in China, about my future assignment. I told him I was working toward a professional license but wouldn't be finished before my return; I needed another year. There were compelling reasons to extend my study leave and finish the licensure process in the U.S. There were equally compelling reasons to return to the field and complete it at a distance. This was back in the days of using phone cards to make long distance calls—not a reliable system—so in the middle of our discussion, we ran out of phone card credit and the call abruptly ended.

I burst into tears. I was returning. It was really going to happen. Of course I was, that had been the plan all along, so why was my reaction so strong? I knew Charlie would call back, and I only had as long as it would take him to scratch off the pin and dial about a zillion numbers. I told myself to pull it together, stop crying, and not let Charlie know I had fallen apart. He did call back, and we hammered out the basic details of the assignment I would have when I returned. It was perfect for me, my interests, my gifts, and yet . . .

This was year twelve into my life as a cross-cultural worker, so the intensity of my response was shocking even to me. I had never heard other cross-cultural workers talk about how much harder it can be to return to the field than to go the first time. It turns out my experience was not unusual. Over the years, I have seen this particular type of finishing well be laced with more grief than other transitions, and because it's unexpected, it becomes harder than it needs to be.

Here we circle back to expectations: because I had made what I thought was the much harder transition of going to the field the first time, complete with quitting my job, leaving a roommate in the lurch, raising support, and storing all my earthly possessions, I expected to be in familiar territory. What I hadn't factored in was the drastic difference between initially going to the field and returning to the field after a home assignment. In short, when I first went, my parents were twelve years younger, I thought my time away would be only for two years, and there were no precious nieces. Adults don't change that much in the length of a term, but children do, and if they're very young, they will forget you. Upon my first foray into the field, while it was hard on my family (especially since communication was either difficult or expensive), we were all adults with normal reactions to my departure. Meaning, there were some tears, but they were laced with excitement and the comfort of knowing I was following God. It was all different when I had to leave the second time. Emily turned six the summer before I returned to China. I had a good bit of traveling to do in the months leading up to my return to the field and every time I prepared to leave for a trip, she screamed, "Are you going to CHINA?!" Her reaction was so visceral that I wondered what impact it would have on her when I did leave for China. I didn't want her to hate the land I loved or worse have a seed of bitterness in her tender heart toward God.

I knew I still needed to live my life and go where God led, but the first time it was done with a level of naiveté. I did not know what it would be like to miss major holidays year after year or the birth of friends' babies or funerals of loved ones. Now I knew, and with the knowledge came a wave of counting the cost that cut more deeply than the first wave. I was more torn because now I had a sense of home on opposite sides of the world—both real and important but so far apart. And yet I was extremely excited about my upcoming assignment. It would tap into many areas of my interests and skills and included the potential to influence many. Most of my life experiences were culminating in the practically perfect job. I was grateful and excited *and* hated hearing my niece scream.

Five questions for those preparing to return to the field after a furlough or home assignment:

1. Were there major changes—either for you or for loved ones—since you first went to the field, such as health problems, births of babies, aging family members, job losses, or financial stress?

2. Were you able to adequately address any marital, parenting, educational, health, or personal issues during your furlough or home assignment?

Your Unique Path

3. Are you returning to a familiar location or assignment? If not, how much do you know about your new home?

4. How was your time in your passport country? Are you looking forward to returning to the field?

5. What is the length of this upcoming commitment?

Subsequent furloughs and home assignments

Five days before a two-month home assignment, I got a call from my sister at a time she should have been sleeping. Instantly I was alarmed. "Amy, I'm at the hospital with Mom. Dad fell and broke his hip. Because of his health complications, the doctors don't know whether to do surgery or not. They are trying to weigh the risk of death during surgery against other treatment options. We don't know much and probably won't until tomorrow. Nothing has to be done immediately, and we'll keep you informed."

My plan for those five days had been to pull together a presentation I was scheduled to give at a conference on Mental Health and Cross-Cultural Workers a few days after I landed in the U.S. I had surveyed over a hundred people in my organization and compiled the results, but I still needed to determine how to convey my findings in a way that would most benefit attendees. My plan was thrown a huge wrench as I was in severe shock for two days after my sister's call. I walked around my apartment with deep thoughts like, "I should wash the dishes." I was unable to focus on anything; I just kept wandering around.

Ultimately the doctors decided to operate, and my dad lived through the surgery, but his femur was broken during the hip replacement surgery. He was moved to rehab the day before I got home. In the midst of all of this, my parents' kitchen was being remodeled, so most of the contents of their kitchen were still scattered around the dining room. The contractors were the ones to help my dad after he fell and had finished the project before I returned to the U.S. Suffice it to say, between the chaos in the house and the attention my dad needed, we were in survival mode. I was able to see Dad for two days before flying off to present at the conference. When I planned and dreamed about my two-month break from the daily stressors of my job and life on the field, it didn't involve this twist. Looking back, however, it was a gift to be a part of family life for which I was usually too far away. It was a gift to help my parents and my sisters and nieces. It was a gift to spend time with my dad as he convalesced. It was a gift, but the curveballs of life did change the flavor of my needed break.

Often subsequent furloughs or home assignments are centered around significant life events, including (1) the graduation of a high schooler and helping him or her adjust to college, (2) a significant family event such as a wedding or fiftieth wedding anniversary, (3) professional development involving further schooling, (4) and health or personal issues that are better addressed "back home."

Five questions for those preparing for subsequent furloughs and home assignments:

1. Because you've been down this path before, take some time to reflect on how your previous furlough(s) or home assignment(s) went. What went well? What changes would you like to make? How are the needs of this furlough or home assignment different from any previous one(s)?

2. How much control do you have over the timing of this furlough or home assignment? Is your agency open to and willing to work around your needs and those of your family?

3. Is what you're facing socially acceptable and typical, such as a child graduating or aging parents? Or are there aspects of your situation that you don't want widely known

or shared? A child in a faith crisis? A spouse experiencing a mental health issue? Some form of unhealthy behavior that needs to be addressed, such as substance abuse, anger management issues, or pornography?

4. Overall, was this past term positive or negative? Are you looking forward to your furlough or home assignment?

5. Regarding your setup while on furlough, do you have housing? A vehicle? How many locations do you need to visit? Will you need to raise additional funds for your next term?

Because graduation and helping a child transition to college is one of the most crucial transitions for a Third Culture Kid (TCK), let's look at this scenario in depth. Here are *five additional questions for high school graduates who will return to their passport country to attend college*:

1. How much time have you spent in your passport country? How connected do you feel to it? Are you able to attend a debriefing for TCKs who are transitioning to college?

2. Overall, how has your time on the field been? Did you have a positive experience? Do you feel your parents were used by God? Do you feel held hostage to their call?

3. Regarding finances, you may have scholarships or help from family to pay for college or you may have needed to take out student loans. Regardless of whether or not you need to take out loans in your own name, you need to begin to take responsibility and ownership for your finances.

4. How clear are you on what you want to do with your life? While many things are uncertain when you go off for college and plans can change, there is a difference in how you

approach entering college when you have a plan versus when your path is unclear. Both pathways can lead to good places, and it is not a given that your interests and major will stay the same. But for you finishing well encompasses your last year of high school and the summer before college, not what you will do after you get to college.

5. What number are you in the family order? The transition from high school to life after high school is always significant, but it is also specifically impacted by birth order. This transition is also about your parents. If you are the first child in your family going off to college, this may be the first major transition your family has gone through since the last child was born. For middle children, your transition marks the continuing change in family dynamics. And if you're the last child in the family, then your graduation may signal the beginning of your parents being empty nesters. Remember that it's not all about you.

Five questions for parents of high school graduates:

1. For high school graduates moving to their passport country to attend college and for their parents, there are several areas of overlap, including distance, finances, majors/plans, and how many children in the family have transitioned from high school. What do these areas look like from your side? If this is not your first child moving out of your home, how is this time different?

2. The one aspect that is going to be significantly different for you as you approach this transition is the personality of *this* child going through *this* transition. Is she an advanced planner and highly disciplined so you don't need to monitor all of the details related to college applications? Or is this child easily distracted and a bit disorganized? Does he resent your input or seek it out? Again, some of these

personality types are certainly easier to work with than others, but none of them are wrong in and of themselves.

3. Think about the life skills that your graduate might need as they transition out of your home abroad and moves to his passport country. The skills needed overseas may have been different from those she will need in their passport country. There are some skills in his passport country he may not have needed to develop growing up overseas. Does she know how to use a washing machine? The basics of laundry and reading labels? Have you talked about handling a credit card and other financial decisions she will be facing? Does he know how to drive and what to do for basic car maintenance?

4. How much of your son or daughter's first year of college will you be able to spend in your passport country? Are other family members living in the area where your child will be attending college?

5. In addition to your own transition, there may be other children still in your home, and you play a role in helping them to prepare for the transition as well. How can you help your other children finish well with this sibling?

Leaving the field for the foreseeable future

And then the day comes, whether at the end of a two-year commitment, four-year term, or after the roots have gone so deep you don't know who you are apart from this life you've been leading. Not surprisingly, for me this was the most costly of all the looming transitions. It cost me my home, my job, my sense of identity, my community, my easy access to friends, my interesting location, and my money. Ultimately, it cost me my beloved shire.

Although I have never given birth, I have known plenty of

pregnant women and even been a birth coach multiple times. My mom said she loved being pregnant except for the last month; she claims the role of the last month is to get you so uncomfortable you are willing to go through anything to birth the baby. This is parallel to the process God took me through before I finally left the field. After many wonderful years on the field, God was loosening my ties to my shire, and at one point I said to myself, "I would rather be unemployed than doing this."

My own sentiment stunned me.

But the starkness was a gift. What had been life-giving was no longer such. What had been a good fit was causing blisters on my soul. I had a choice to make. Was I going to stay and live on the outside while dying on the inside, or was I going to leave? If you've lived overseas, I know you get it. You get the agony this moment brings. When you see the insurmountable needs around you and the unending nature of the work, and you believe strongly in the work, that which should be an easy decision for me was still agonizing. I had been asking God for several years to release me. Part of me was perplexed why he wouldn't, but deep inside I knew it was for my own good. If I left the field too early, there was too much potential for a seed of bitterness to take root. Not long after I hit my rock-bottom moment of desiring unemployment over my current situation, I was cruising home from a friend's in the back seat of a taxi one glorious August night when God whispered, "You can go. This will be your last year."

Relieved and sad.

Hopeful and lost.

Curious about the future and annoyed it wouldn't be in China.

Ready for a new challenge and confused how an organization that had once been such a good fit no longer was.

Happy to be moving near family again and sad not to watch teammates' kids grow up.

Your story of leaving the field will be just that, your story—colored by the teammates you've had, the land you've lived in, the work you've done, and the personality God has given you.

Your Unique Path

But maybe you've seen echoes of your story within the details of my story.

Five questions for those leaving the field for the foreseeable future:

1. How long have you been in your country of service? Overall, how was your time there? How satisfying was the work? Are you able to participate in a debriefing and renewal program after you leave the field?

2. Regarding reasons for leaving the field, we all have the public reason we give and our real reason. Often, the public and the real reason are one and the same. But in your case, it might not be appropriate to share the real reason publicly. Does it involve crisis? Where and with whom can you share?

3. How abrupt was the ending? Were you able to prepare for your departure in a timely fashion? Or were there political or health factors that dictated a quick departure?

4. Regarding your organization's policies, how long will you be able to stay on support and have access to insurance and salaries? Are the policies able to flex with the needs of your situation?

5. Do you have a sense of what's next? Will you still be associated with your organization?

This chapter has made me want to crawl into my bed and never come out. The amount of transitions you will experience when called to the field can be overwhelming. Locations change, families change, jobs change, marital status changes, children graduate and change, organizations change, churches change, the countries you live in and love change.

And you change.

Looming Transitions

It might make you wonder if the foundation you have built your life upon will eventually change as well. The writer of Hebrews assures us Jesus is the same yesterday, today, and forever. Yes, this season will change. And sadly, no, it will not be the last change you face. But you can be comforted with the knowledge that you have resources and support in God, in others, and in yourself. While it may be tempting (and even necessary for short periods of time) to hide under the covers, ultimately you will have to face the stark reality that change is coming. You need to remind yourself that with the pain of this season dying come blessings as space is created for something new to be born in your soul.

Grace and peace to you in light of your looming transition. May the God of all comfort help you finish well.

Acknowledgements

I love to read acknowledgments because of the snapshot they provide into a writer's world and process. When I set out to write *Looming Transitions* I was still living and serving in China and had no idea I was writing myself through the largest transition—up to this point—in my life. Nor did I grasp as I typed my goal of 500 words a day how many people would be involved in this process. I am grateful, humbled, and happy to have met so many along the way. This is a labor of love, frustration, community, isolation, surprise, tears, and celebration and I couldn't have done it without many, many.

To my family who knew me before the idea of cross-cultural service was even on the radar. In the days before email and when phone calls cost an arm and a leg, you sent me off to China guilt free. I knew you'd miss me, but you never made me feel I had to choose between you and a life of overseas service. You helped me fly high while staying rooted in parts of American culture I love. Elizabeth, remember subscribing to *Sports Illustrated* and mailing it to me every week? Laura, I cannot tell you how much it meant to me when Grandma died that you called and retold me the entire service and the conversation you had with every person. You know I thrive on details and I cannot imagine what that phone call cost. Mom, you were the friend of the library and if there was a patron saint to mailing books, her name would be Marsha Young. Dad, you're no longer with us, yet your fingerprints are all over my story. Though technology is wonderful, I miss the days when you'd call and read me the entire March Madness brackets over the phone. And then call back in subsequent weeks as we worked our way through the tournament. Thank you that you each came to see me and understand the land I love.

Del, Sue, Emily, Katy, Anna, and Chloe, your love and interest leads the parade on "how to love a family member overseas." Thank you. You've also been so supportive as I've muddled my way back to the States. I love you.

Amy, your friendship has helped anchor me to myself. You knew me before I went to China. You knew me while I was in China. You know me now, post China. You help me feel normal and defined by more than a place. Phillip Yancey's book title *Soul Survivor* is what you and Bill have done for me—helped my soul survive. I love how you have opened your home and family to me again and again.

Kim, who would have guessed when our paths crossed in Lewis Hall so many years ago, the ways our lives would be woven together. I love that we have gotten to see each other in our homes around the world as we have learned about culture, God, and life. I'm thankful Steve has joined in our international journeys!

Marla, you get my quirky side and I cannot watch the start of a *Friends* episode without thinking of you. The two years we were roommates are the two years I point to in my adult experience as being "normal." Enough said.

Lisa, you read my mind. I will send you an email or recount a conversation and you have the uncanny ability to respond with perfection. If I'm annoyed, you're annoyed on my behalf; if I'm happy, you peg the point of greatest joy; if I'm sad, you pass the Kleenex. You speak the dialect of *what the LDL,* Chicken, thinking outside the box, and aunthood (which spell check is wanting to correct to "adult hood"). My world dimmed a bit when you left Beijing.

My China people. I want to list all of your names. Everyone of you I met over the years. This book would not have been possible if you had not done life with me. I'm so afraid I'll forget a name and as I sit here thinking of you, I am flooded by the richness of life with you. I miss you. I'm grateful for most of my experienc-

Acknowledgements

es with you ☺. I'd like to share how each of you influenced me, but that would be another book. Erin, Shelley, Becky, Stephanie, Joann, Cassi, Liesl, Erin, Dae, Charlie, Joy, Daniel, Nathan, Mike, Anne (again and again you are woven into these pages), Isabel, Gabe, Nate, Tommy, Jon, Paula, Becca, Daniel, Mikkin, Karl, Tobiah (and now Esther), Mike, Wendy, Tom, Sandy, John Mark, Sue, Matt, Sally, Katrina, Maddie, Cathy, Sherri, Frank, Ginny, Pam, Brian, Nick, Kim, Jonathan, Rachel, Samantha, Maddie, Elisa, Patty, Sam, Paul, Ben, Sarah, Shelley, Ben, Bridget, Brooke, Andy, Huang Shan, Jenny, Michael, Grace, Xiao Zhang, Gilda, Ashley, Renee, Tim, LeAnne, Lee, Jason, Lisa, Kristina, Michelle, Michelle, Dan, Jenny, Nathan, and Katie. And this is just the tip of the iceberg!

To Velvet Ashes. Danielle, when you contacted me with this dream, we didn't know you were birthing my future as well. I love the editors team of Danielle Wheeler, Patty Stallings, and Kimberly Todd. Working with you inspires me to lean into God, community, and knowing myself more. I wrote this book and then put it away for two years. Velvet Ashes, it is through knowing you and seeing a need, I pulled it out and reworked it (and reworked it and reworked it). Thank you for being a group who loves Jesus, connections, seeing people's lives change, and have hearts big enough for the joys, sorrows, struggles, and celebrations of life. You are my people, and I am yours.

Tanya Marlow. Your name is a full sentence because in you is fullness. God has used you as the bridge to so much in my life. Even though we've never gotten to meet in person, you have enhanced my life beyond what I thought an "internet friendship" could! I met you while I still lived in China and began to hope that friendship would be possible for me with those who would never know my China side. Being a part of The Inkwell, the online community of writers and creatives you formed, is a taste of heaven because it is a space of diversity and love. As are you. (Shout out to the Inkwell!)

David Rupert, when Jim Walters introduced us at the Bear Clause writers group and you told me how I was doing so much wrong when it came to blogging, I wondered "Who is this guy?!" Well, it turns out, one who has become a dear, dear friend. As I've returned to the States and become more involved in the writing community, thank you for befriending me. I love our annual writer's conference and Writer's on the Rock. And you were right about my blogging. I'm glad I listened to you. But more than that, I'm glad I know you.

Jim Walters, this book is because you said to me, "Write a book." It was the time and God used your words in that moment. Thank you for championing me.

I had no idea that an editor could be an advocate and then I met Deb Hall. Deb, you showed me that you got the vision of this book and that through editing and rewriting, it could be what it has become. Thank you seems inadequate when you met my ramblings and overuse of the words *"just, things,* and *that,"* with loving nudges towards clarity. You helped me see the Holy Spirit as my life editor. If he can do in my life what you have done in my writing, I have hope for us all!

Theresa Board, you were the surprise gift in this whole process. Other gifts I knew I needed and went out searching for them. You, you are God's gift to me. When I said on my author's Facebook page that I was looking for someone to edit my book with fresh eyes and you responded, I didn't know you. You took a risk and me and I took a risk on you and look how far we've come! The day you emailed me, maybe around chapter 4, that you were editing it under a towel at the pool while your kids swam and you couldn't see the computer screen without the towel because of the sun—I'm not exaggerating—I felt my heart expand in my chest. You more than edited, you commented about parts that connected with you and how this information would help people. Thank you for being the gift that keeps giving.

Kay Bruner, when I picture your role in this book, I see a snowy path. You walked down it before me and I have put my foot every place you stepped first. I know there are people who would turn around and say, "Shoo!! Go make your own path.

Acknowledgements

Do not follow me." Instead, every single time I contacted you, you said, "This is how I did it." I found out who did your cover and contacted Christie Kim. She is, as you all can tell, amazing! The formatting and computer part freaked me out and Andy Bruner who helped you, his wife, because he's your husband, helped me simply because he is one of the kindest people. You have offered me nothing but friendship and kindness and suggestions in some of the chapters. In a world that thrives on scarcity and competition, you have been generosity and connection. Thank you!

To my small group in Denver. It is not an easy thing to leave a life and a community. But knowing you were waiting for me and every other Friday night would open your homes and lives to me, softened the bumps on my landing back in a land I was surprised to be living in. I love our group!

And finally to new friends who remind me that Looming Transitions will not always loom. As Anne of Green Gables said, "Kindred spirits are not as scarce as I used to think. It's splendid to find out there are so many of them in the world."

Now to Him who is able to do immeasurably more than all we ask or imagine, according to His power that is at work within us, to Him be glory in the church and in Christ Jesus throughout all generations, for ever and ever! Amen.

Ephesians 3:20-21

About the Author

Amy Young lived in Asia for twenty years, helping hundreds of people adjust to the field and prepare to leave it. She's on the leadership team of Velvet Ashes (www.velvetashes.com)—an online community for women in cross-cultural service. She blogs regularly at The Messy Middle (www.messymiddle.com). You may also be interested in purchasing a downloadable PDF of this book and a downloadable Looming Transitions Workbook at www.gumroad.com/amyyoung.

Amazon chooses to promote books based on the number of reviews. Would you consider writing a short review for Looming Transitions on Amazon?

Endnotes

1. Bob Buford, Finishing Well: What People Who Really Live Do Differently (Nashville, TN: Integrity Publishers, 2004).

2. Names have been changed in these examples.

3. "A Quote by Carlos Castaneda," Goodreads, https://www.goodreads.com/quotes/2415-the-trick-is-in-what-one-emphasizes-we-either-make. Accessed September 8, 2014.

4. Matthew 23:14-30, NIV

5. Donald Miller, Through Painted Deserts: Light, God, and Beauty on the Open Road (Nashville, TN: Thomas Nelson Publishers, 2005), x.

6. This might sound harsh. This is why we all need to be aware of what we are "putting out there" during transition. I have found people to be unbelievably kind and understanding of the stress people are under in transitions; but there comes a point when repeated comments of "war and death so that you can be with your boyfriend" will wear even the most patient down.

7. Kermit is famous to American's around my age. He's a frog muppet who sang a song called *It's Not Easy Being Green*.

8. Doc Childre and Howard Martin as quoted in Donna Karlin, "Perspectives: Stress . . . . The Body and Mind's Response," http://betterperspective.blogspot.com/2005/05/stress-the-body-and-minds-response.html. Accessed August 20, 2015.

9. For more information on managing and setting expectations see: David Alev, "Managing Expectations - Part 1 - Learn-

ing How to Manage Expectations Is a Critical Consulting Skill," http://consultingacademy.com/a08.shtm. Accessed January 23, 2011.

10. Frank Muller and Richard A. Coughlin. "The Influence of One's Expectations on behavior," http://adrr.com/adr4/expect.htm. Accessed January 23, 2011.

11. "Expectations and Hidden Issues," http://www.positive-way.com/hidden.htm.Accessed January 23, 2011.

12. Archibald Hart, "Stress and Anxiety," Focus on the Family http://media.focusonthefamily.com/topicinfo/stress_and_anxiety.pdf. Accessed January 25, 2011.

13. Elizabeth Scott, "Common Symptoms of Too Much Stress," http://stress.about.com/od/understandingstress/a/stress_symptoms.htm. Accessed January 25, 2011.

14. "Common Stress Reactions A Self-Assessment," https://www.omh.ny.gov/omhweb/disaster_resources/pandemic_influenza/doctors_nurses/Common_Stress_Reactions.html. Accessed May 19, 2015.

15. John Donne, "No Man Is An Island Poem," Poemhunter.com, http://www.poemhunter.com/poem/no-man-is-an-island. Accessed May 19, 2015.

16. Deuteronomy 6:2 NIV

17. John Ortberg, *God Is Closer Than You Think: If God Is Always with Us, Why Is He so Hard to Find?* (Grand Rapids, Mich.: Zondervan, 2005).

18. Ibid., 120.

19. https://www.youtube.com/watch?v=IoIc4c42-ro

20. If you'd like to explore this further, you can take a spiritual pathways inventory at https://classes.willowcreek.org/Content/HtmlImages/Public/Documents/General/HowToHear.SpiritualPathwaysAssessment.pdf.

21. "Home: Yahoo Answers," http://answers.yahoo.com/question/index?qid=20080526051638AA5NoTt. Accessed February 17, 2011.

22. "Definition: Revive," Merriam-Webster, http://www.merriam-webster.com/dictionary/revive. Accessed February 17, 2011.

23. Just like Mary Tyler Moore as she threw her hat in the air!

24. If for no other reason than we are done with grammar. I thought you could use a laugh if you actually checked this footnote. I received the following text from my sister: "I had to clarify to your youngest niece 'Aunt Amy has a strong *sense* of smell, not a strong smell.'"

25. Often in Western countries contracts hold greater weight than they do in some Asian countries; in those countries the relationship holds greater weight. In this case, my friends had no relationship with the moving company.

26. If you have kids or teens in the house, remember to have age appropriate expectations as to how they live with and process tension and stress.

27. "A Quote by Mark Twain," Goodreads, https://www.goodreads.com/quotes/677018-climate-is-what-we-expect-weather-is-what-we-get. Accessed June 25, 2015.

28. "A Quote by Patrick Young on Trouble and Weather," http://blog.gaiam.com/quotes/authors/patrick-young/27789. Accessed June 25, 2015.

29. Brené Brown, The Gifts of Imperfection: Let Go of Who You Think You're Supposed to Be and Embrace Who You Are (Center City, MN.: Hazelden, 2010), 72.

30. My dad had eleven aunts and uncles, many of whom didn't have children so my childhood was filled with "the greats and the grands" as I called them. I was incredibly blessed to have only one grandparent die while I was in high school and the other three lived until I was in my twenties and thirties.

31. John 3:30 NIV

32. Brian Fort, "Thank You Is Not Enough." Developing a Champion Care Strategy. Bear Valley Church, Lakewood. July 8, 2015. Speech.

33. For example, you may live in a hot climate and be moving to a cold area that won't have long underwear your size.

34. Panos Kourtis, "The Impact of the Transitional Object in an Art Therapy Setting for Elderly Immigrant People with Long Term and Enduring Mental Health Problems Living in Care Homes in Scotland," http://www.academia.edu/6952987/Research_ProThe_impact_of_the_transitional_object_in_an_Art_therapy_setting_for_elderly_immigrant_people_with_long_term_and_enduring_mental_health_problems_living_in_care_homes_in_Scotland.posal_.Accessed July 9, 2015.

35. I know you could point out it was "objects" given that it was more than one picture frame. Transition can make people feisty. I think you get my point that I limited myself to a relatively small box.

36. Charles E. Hummel, *Tyranny of the Urgent*. Rev. and Expanded. ed. (Downers Grove, Ill.: InterVarsity, 1994).

37. He was the president of our organization and I've changed his name.

38. Brené C. Brown, *The Gifts of Imperfection: Let Go of Who You Think You're Supposed to Be and Embrace Who You Are* (Center City, MN: Hazelden, 2010), 72.

39. Gary D. Chapman, *The Five Love Languages: How to Express Heartfelt Commitment to Your Mate* (Chicago: Northfield Pub., 1992).

40. Donald Miller, *Through Painted Deserts: Light, God, and Beauty on the Open Road* (Nashville, TN: Thomas Nelson, 2005).

41. "Island Ireland: Irish Blessings & Prayers," Island Ireland: Irish Blessings & Prayers, http://islandireland.com/Pages/folk/sets/bless.html. Accessed July 16, 2015.

42. John Ortberg, *Soul Keeping: Caring for the Most Important Part of You* (Grand Rapids, Mich.: Zondervan, 2014). Chapter 13.

43. 1 Thessalonians 4:13 NASB

44. Philippians 2:12 NIV

45. "Strong's Greek: 2716. κατεργάζομαι (katergazomai) -- to Work out," *Strong's Greek: 2716. κατεργάζομαι (katergazomai) -- to Work out*, from http://biblehub.com/greek/2716.htm. Accessed July 27, 2015.

46. Barbara Kingsolver, *The Poisonwood Bible: A Novel* (New York: HarperFlamingo, 1998), 492.

47. C. S. Lewis, *The Pilgrim's Regress; an Allegorical Apology for Christianity, Reason, and Romanticism* (Grand Rapids: Eerdmans, 1959), 198.

48. Genesis 12:1 NIV

Made in the USA
Columbia, SC
16 July 2018